THE
FIELD&
STREAM
BOWHUNTING
HANDBOOK
NEW AND REVISED

The *Field & Stream* Fishing and Hunting Library

Hunting

The Field & Stream *Bowhunting Handbook*, by Bob Robb

The Field & Stream *Deer Hunting Handbook*, by Jerome B. Robinson

The Field & Stream *Firearms Safety Handbook*, by Doug Painter

The Field & Stream *Shooting Sports Handbook*, by Thomas McIntyre

The Field & Stream *Turkey Hunting Handbook*, by Philip Bourjaily

The Field & Stream *Upland Bird Hunting Handbook*, by Bill Tarrant

Fishing

The Field & Stream *Baits and Rigs Handbook*, by C. Boyd Pfeiffer

The Field & Stream *Bass Fishing Handbook*,
   by Mark Sosin and Bill Dance

The Field & Stream *Fishing Knots Handbook*, by Peter Owen

The Field & Stream *Fly Fishing Handbook*, by Leonard M. Wright, Jr.

The Field & Stream *Tackle Care and Repair Handbook*,
   by C. Boyd Pfeiffer

THE

FIELD&STREAM

BOWHUNTING

HANDBOOK

NEW AND REVISED

BOB ROBB

The Lyons Press
Guilford, Connecticut
An imprint of The Globe Pequot Press

The Lyons Press is an imprint of The Globe Pequot Press.

Printed in The United States of America

10 9 8 7 6 5 4 3 2

Design by Mimi LaPoint

ISBN 978-1-59921-089-6

The Library of Congress previously cataloged an earlier (paperback) edition as follows:

Robb, Bob
    The Field & stream bowhunting handbook / Robert Robb.
cm. — (Field & stream fishing and hunting library)
    Includes index.
    ISBN 1-55821-914-5
    1. Bowhunting.   I. Title. II. Title: Field & stream bowhunting handbook. III. Title: Field and stream bowhunting handbook.
IV. Series.
SK36.R63   1999
    799.2'028'5—dc21   99-10281
                                    CIP

CONTENTS

CONTENTS

INTRODUCTION

If, when hunting, your need to kill an animal supersedes all other reasons for being afield, bowhunting is not for you. If you have time to read only the condensed version of a great novel, and not the entire novel itself, bowhunting is not for you. If you feel right at home in today's go-go world, where life rushes by at light speed and you can't take time to smell the roses, bowhunting is not for you. If being alone makes you uncomfortable or if having the success or failure of a project resting solely on your shoulders is discomforting, bowhunting is not for you.

If, on the other hand, you love a challenge, bowhunting just might be for you. If you treasure things that require commitment and dedication, bowhunting just might be for you. If you like going it alone, with no one else to blame should something go wrong, bowhunting just might be for you. If you enjoy being in the woods, feeling it, smelling it, living and breathing it, bowhunting might be for you. If the most important thing about hunting to you is not to kill an animal every time out but instead the joy of the hunt itself, the chance to get close to animals and learn as much about them as you can, then bowhunting might be for you.

Bowhunting has been called the ultimate hunting challenge. There's good reason for that. By its very nature, bowhunting is a close-range, smell-their-breath discipline. To consistently get close enough to any game animal for a quality bow shot requires a high degree of woodsmanship, the type not often needed by firearms hunters, who regularly fill their tags with shots well over a football field in length. There's an old saying in bowhunting that goes something like this: "When the hunt's over with a rifle it's just beginning with a bow." As a rifle hunter, I know that if I can just see the animal I want he's probably mine, no matter how far away he is. But with a bow, finding him is just the beginning. So many things can go wrong between sighting the animal and finally loosing an arrow that it is never, ever a sure thing.

It is this challenge that has stimulated the recent explosion in bowhunters across America, who today number close to 3 million. Bowhunting success can never be measured with a stack of punched tags, a freezer full of venison, or a wall full of antlers. Instead, it is measured as much in attitude as ability. Successful bowhunters must be committed to the sport, because there are no shortcuts. It takes time to hone shooting skills, pare down hunting equipment, and comprehend that, most times out, there will be no shooting. It takes time to learn the habits and haunts of the magnificent game animals we hunt, so getting that close-range opportunity is not simply a matter of luck, but one of skill.

This book is designed to help you get started bowhunting. The foundation for success in the field is based upon two large building blocks. One—your own attitude, desire, and commitment—cannot be learned from any book. It's up to you. The other—the selection of the right bowhunting equipment, and the basics of how to use it—you can learn about in these pages. Here we'll help you make wise equipment choices designed to make you the most effective bow shot you can be in the field, under hunting conditions. We'll also give you some basic hunting advice, from how to dress to how to get into position for a shot, and then how to make that shot when the chips are down.

Perhaps the best piece of advice the beginner could take from these pages is this: Spend some time at your local archery pro shop. There you'll find friendly, skilled people who can help you select the right equipment for the challenges of local bowhunting, provide instruction on how to use it, and offer service when your gear needs it. Just as important, you'll meet area bow-hunters who come to the shop as much to chew the fat and hang around with others cut from the same cloth as to shoot a few arrows. These men and women are, by and large, the finest people I've ever met. Most are free with advice and willing to help a beginner get started. If you're not careful, you'll find yourself enrolled in a shooting league, spending weekends at local tournaments and fun shoots, and, when you're not shooting, spending more of your free time raising money for, and investing sweat equity in, wildlife habitat improvements and the health of game herds.

Soon you'll be trading bowhunting stories with friends. Unlike hunting tales told by firearms hunters, which usually center around game taken, 9 times out of 10 bowhunting stories begin with phrases like, "Man, if he would have only taken *one more step* . . ."; "I crawled on that buck for over an hour trying to get a shot, and just when I was getting into range the wind switched and that was that!"; or "He was so close I could have reached out and touched him, but the brush was just too thick. Next year I'm going to get him. . . ." They are tales of challenges met head on, where a shot was *almost* taken, but things just weren't quite right. These are stories not of finality, but of hopes and dreams of tomorrow. For bowhunters, the hunt never ends.

When it all does come together and the arrow flies straight and true, there's a feeling of pride and accomplishment like few others I've ever known. It doesn't matter whether it was a buck with big antlers or a fat doe for the larder. The smile on the face of a successful bowhunter can light up the night.

Yes, bowhunting can be addictive. There is so much more to it than grabbing a rifle out of the gun case the day before the season opens, filling a tag the first hour of the first day, then forgetting about it until next year. Bowhunters live and breathe their discipline 365 days a year.

Are you ready to make the commitment? Then let's get started.

CHOOSING THE HUNTING BOW

Hunting with a bow and arrow used to be the simplest of sports. All you needed was a recurve or longbow, a back quiver full of cedar arrow shafts fletched with real turkey feathers and tipped with a large broadhead that took some hand sharpening, a leather shooting glove, and a farm with deer on it.

Today, you still need the deer-infested farm, but other than that the face of bowhunting has changed dramatically since the late 1960s, when the first reasonably priced compound bows became available. Walk into any well-stocked archery pro shop today and you'll approach sensory overload among the endless array of high-tech compound bows, arrow shafts, broadheads, bow sights, and other accessories.

But it all centers around the bow. Obviously, before you begin bowhunting you'll need a bow of some sort. The question is, How do you sort through all the hype and choices to find the right one for you?

M. R. James, one of the founders and former editor of *Bowhunter* magazine, once wrote that choosing a hunting bow was a lot like choosing a wife—it all boiled down to a matter of individual taste. His observation is still right on the money. Virtually every major bow manufacturer in business today builds top-notch hunting bows. There are subtle differences, though, and how they look and feel in your hand and how they shoot for you may not be the same as how they look, feel, and shoot for your best hunting buddy. Selecting a new bow is a personal decision, one that should be based on your own tastes and tempered with an objective look at performance and cost.

TRADITIONAL VERSUS COMPOUND BOWS

During the early days of the compound bow—the late 1960s and early 1970s—virtually all archers began their careers shooting either a longbow or recurve—"traditional" bows—then stepped up to a compound bow. Today just the opposite is true. Beginners start with a compound that lets them master the skills needed to

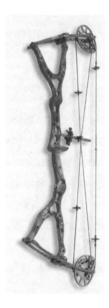

The BowTech Guardian is a prime example of a high-tech compound bow. It features an elongated aluminum riser, a center-tracking cam design that eliminates cam lean and limb torque, split parallel limbs, and a center-pivot design. When affixed with a modern hunting sight, arrow rest, and bow quiver, it will produce tight arrow groups under the most demanding hunting conditions.

become a good shot before ever thinking about stepping back in time and shooting a traditional bow.

That's not to say that traditional bows are no longer good for anything. I know serious traditional archers who have track records that would make the best compound shooters green with envy. It's just that it takes much more time, effort, and commitment to become a skilled "instinctive" shooter with unsighted traditional bows than it does to become proficient with a compound bow. If, after you've achieved basic shooting skills with a compound bow, the thought of emulating the original archers tickles your fancy, then go ahead and try your hand at traditional archery. But not before.

COMPOUND BOWS: WHAT ARE THEY?

Simply stated, a compound bow uses a system of round or eccentric wheels and cables that work together as the bowstring is pulled back to reduce a given bow's "holding weight" well below its listed "draw weight." This is a huge advantage that is unavailable to the shooter using a traditional bow. Here's how it works.

With a traditional bow the shooter draws the bowstring back, reaching the bow's peak draw weight—the heaviest amount of pressure needed to draw the string back—at full draw. There he must hold it on his fingers until he's ready to release the arrow. Let's say that is 70 pounds. That's a lot of weight! With a compound bow, however, the shooter gets a distinct advantage from the wheels and cables. A compound bow with a peak draw weight of the same 70 pounds and a "let-off" of 65 percent also forces the shooter to put 70 pounds of pressure on his fingers as the bow is drawn back to about the halfway point. Then, this 70-pound peak weight is slowly reduced as the shooter continues to pull the bowstring all the way back to full draw, where he has to hold only 35 percent of the bow's peak draw weight on his fingers until the time of release. That's only 24.5 pounds of pressure! With such reduced pressure on your fingers, you'll be able to aim longer at the target without muscle fatigue, meaning you'll shoot more accurately.

In the early days of compound bows, the common let-off was about 50 percent. Today, let-offs typically fall between 65 and 80 percent. High let-off bows are increasingly popular, despite the fact that for many years the Pope & Young Club did not allow animals taken with bows with a let-off above 65 percent into their record book. But today more compound hunting bows are sold with let-offs higher than 65 percent than at or below this figure. Recognizing this trend, Pope & Young now allows record-book entries of animals taken with compound bows with a let-off of 80 percent or lower.

Compounds have other advantages over traditional bows. For one thing, they allow you to shoot a faster arrow, which reduces trajectory, which in turn makes it easier to hit a target at unknown distances. They also generate more kinetic energy, which helps a broadhead-tipped arrow penetrate more deeply. And modern compound bows are designed for use with the latest high-tech accessories, such as bow sights, arrow rests, and release aids that foster precise shooting at distances traditional archers can only dream about. It's no wonder that more than 90 percent of all modern bowhunters shoot a compound bow.

Here, then, are things you'll need to know as you go about selecting that new compound bow.

DOMINANT EYE

The first decision you'll have to make is whether to shoot your bow right- or left-handed. This is not a function of whether you *are* right- or left-handed, but whether you're right- or left-eye dominant. Normally the dominant eye is on the same side of the body as the dominant hand, but not always. Here's how to find out.

Hold your hands at arm's length, and then form a small hole between the thumbs and forefingers. Keep both eyes open and center a distant object through this hole. Slowly draw your hands toward your face while staying focused on the object in the center of the hole. Your hands will naturally come back to your dominant eye.

DRAW LENGTH

The most important thing you can do when choosing a compound bow is to select one with *exactly* the right draw length for you. Draw length is defined as the distance from the bowstring at full draw to the back of the bow handle (the side farthest away from you as you hold the bow). A common mistake many bowhunters make is choosing a bow with a draw length that's too long for them. This creates shooting problems, and it won't permit you to shoot to your accuracy potential.

You can gauge your draw length in a couple of ways. But the best method is to pull a bow with a light draw weight to full draw with a long arrow on the bowstring. Anchor it using the same anchor point you'll use when shooting, and have a friend mark the shaft at the back of the bow handle. To find your optimum draw length, measure the shaft from that mark to the string groove on the arrow's nock. (Draw length does not equal the arrow length you'll need, however, so don't confuse the two.) Most archery pro shops have extra-long arrow shafts designed for this purpose. Their equipment and expertise will help you precisely determine your correct draw length.

Your draw length will vary according to whether you shoot with a release aid or your fingers. You'll also find that your draw length may change over time as you become more comfortable shooting compound bows. A good rule of thumb is that you'll shoot more accurately under hunting conditions with a bow set for a draw length that's slightly on the short side. For example, my draw length is 29 inches, but I shoot compound hunting bows with a draw length of 28 1/2 inches.

DRAW WEIGHT

Draw weight is defined as the maximum level of force needed to draw the bow back to the full or cocked position. Modern compound bows come from the factory with draw weights that can be adjusted between a range of 10 to 15 pounds. The two most common are bows with draw weights between 55 and 70 pounds and 65 and 80 pounds. These bows can be adjusted within that draw-weight range to whatever setting the archer chooses.

A few years ago, when compound bow design was not as efficient as it is today, it was necessary to draw a lot of weight to shoot a reasonably fast arrow. Back then many bowhunters were pulling 75 to 85 pounds. Today, however, bows are much more mechanically efficient, and coupled with today's modern arrow shaft design, they produce faster arrow flight with less draw weight and with comparable kinetic energy. For example, with hunting arrows it's easy to achieve a raw arrow speed of between 250 and 280 feet per second today with a draw weight of just 55 to 65 pounds. That's plenty of speed for most bowhunting situations.

That's not to say that raw arrow speed isn't important in bowhunting. It is, especially when shooting at game at unknown distances. A faster arrow has a flatter trajectory, which means you have more leeway in judging the exact distance to the target. The problem is that when you pull more draw weight than you can comfortably handle you sacrifice bow control, which is the real key to accurate shooting. If you have to strain to pull the bow back you'll have tense, taut muscles, which make it more difficult to relax and "lay them in there."

To measure the correct draw weight for you, take these simple tests. Standing flat-footed, hold the bow at arm's length and pull it back. If you have to "cheat"—lift the bow up above your head—to achieve full draw, it's too heavy. Next, do the same thing from a seated position, as if you were sitting in a tree stand. Finally, do it from a kneeling position. Being able to draw your bow with a minimum of movement, even from weird angles, is important when bowhunting. Extra body movement can spook an animal, so the less the better.

WHEELS AND CAMS

Modern compound bows have two wheels, or cams, one at each end of the bow limb. For many years there were three basic and popular designs used by bowhunters, each offering advantages and disadvantages.

The first compound bows actually featured a system that employed four or six wheels. As the basic design evolved, two round wheels became the standard design. The old round-wheel bows were smooth to draw, quiet, and quite accurate. However, round wheels provided relatively slower arrow speeds, and bow makers continued to improve wheel designs to achieve a higher mechanical advantage—and thus more raw arrow speed.

Next came the full, or hard, cam, an egg-shaped eccentric that stored a much higher amount of energy than simple round wheels and therefore produced much faster arrow flight. For that reason they became very popular with bowhunters. The downside to early bows featuring two hard cams was that they produced a lot of vibration at the shot, which made them quite noisy. They were also the most difficult design to consistently tune and, for the average archer, to shoot accurately.

Soon after hard cams became the rage, bow makers began offering what they called a "half cam" design. Half-cams were a compromise, with part of the design round, part egg-shaped. This design produces a smoothness and reliability comparable to that of a round wheel and also provided increased arrow speed, though not as much as that of a hard cam. Half-cams are an excellent choice for bowhunters, and many hunting-bow makers continue to use a variation of this basic design.

Today, however, the most popular hunting-bow design is the single cam or one-cam. Instead of utilizing two identical wheels or cams, one-cam bows have an oversized energy-storing cam on the lower limb and a concentric wheel, called an idler, on the top limb. The advantage of the one-cam design is that it eliminates the problem of wheel timing, an important but difficult-to-control factor in bow tuning. (See Chapter 7 for more information about bow tuning.)

In the beginning, one-cam bows did not produce the raw arrow speed of two-cam designs. However, today's one-cam bows are nearly as fast as comparable two-cam models. In addition,

One-cam bows like this Diamond Black Ice have become increasingly popular in recent years. These bows feature an oversized energy-storing cam on the bottom limb and a roundish "idler" wheel on the top limb.

they are super quiet, feature a high let-off of between 65 and 85 percent, promote level nock travel (an often overlooked but very important part of ultra-accurate arrow flight), and are inherently accurate. For these and other reasons more one-cam bows are currently sold to bowhunters and competitive target archers than any other design.

BOW HANDLES

Bow handles are generally made of aluminum or magnesium, two light, strong metals. Modern handles feature an offset, or cutout, design, which makes it easier for the arrow fletching and broadhead blades to clear the riser during the shot.

The most important thing a bow handle can do for you is feel comfortable in your hand. Some shooters sand or file a handle down a bit to fit their hand more precisely. Others add tape, premade plastic, or wooden grips to alter the feel. When you are shopping for a new bow, pick up several and see how each one feels in your hand. The bow that feels best is generally the one you'll shoot best.

BOW LIMBS

Bow limbs come in straight and recurve designs. Both work equally well, the only difference being how you like their looks. Two basic limb materials are used today—laminated wood and fiberglass. Generally speaking, glass limbs are the most dependable and trouble-free. However, wood limbs are excellent, too, and weigh a bit less. You can't go wrong with either material.

For many years, bow limbs were of a solid design, but today many manufacturers are building bows with "split limbs." On a split-limb bow the center sections of the upper and lower limbs are removed. This creates a lighter bow than the solid-limb design. Some manufacturers claim that split-limbs also reduce noise and increase arrow speed slightly. Others say that split-limb bows are less reliable than solid-limb bows, more difficult to tune, and not as consistent. I predominately hunt with bows featuring solid limbs, but I have a fair amount of experience with split-limb bows and have found that modern versions are very accurate and reliable. To each his own.

As compound design has continued to evolve, bow risers have gotten longer and limbs shorter. Today many manufacturers use what they call "parallel" limbs. These short limbs are so-named because at full draw they bend into a position that is nearly parallel to the ground. At the shot, parallel limbs travel less distance than longer limbs, which allows them to work more in synch with each other. They also produce less vibration, which results in less shock and less noise. They are conducive to very fast arrow flight as well.

STRINGS AND CABLES

A bowstring has two main purposes: to transfer energy from your arms and back muscles to the limbs of the bow and to then transfer that stored energy from the bow to the arrow. Just like with a golf club or tennis racket, this thrust propels the projectile (golf ball, tennis ball, or arrow) and gives it direction. It must transfer energy efficiently and consistently for many hundreds of shots. If the string doesn't meet these criteria, accurate shooting will be impossible.

Two bowstring terms are frequently misused and incorrectly interchanged: "stretch" and "creep." The proper and accurate definition of stretch is the temporary or recoverable elongation of the string caused by the shooting force of the bow.

This is similar to what happens when you pull on a rubber band. Creep is the continual and permanent elongation of the string caused by the load or tension from the bow limbs. This is akin to being hooked up to a torture rack and having your arms and legs pulled in opposite directions for months. One important thing to remember is that with most strings it takes about 200 shots for the material to creep into the manufacturer's specified length. That's why it is important to shoot a new bow at least 200 to 250 times before doing your final fine-tuning and sighting-in.

For many years, Dacron was the material of choice for bow-strings and metal was used in cable systems. In 1985 Brownell & Co. introduced a synthetic material called Fast Flite (technically known as "Spectra"), which is stronger and stretches less. This, in turn, gives us more arrow speed and less problems with wear and breakage. Today most bow companies offer complete Fast Flite string-and-cable systems. Another string material, Vectran, sold by both BCY Fibers and Brownell, does not stretch or creep over time as Fast Flite will, although it is a bit less tolerant to abrasion. Both are excellent choices.

Many top bow makers offer their bows with excellent bow-strings. However, as is the case with all things in life, not all bowstrings are created equal. Many top tournament archers and bowhunters now use custom-made strings. The leading maker is Winner's Choice, whose strings and cables are constructed with a unique process that pre-elongates the string fibers so your string and cables stay at the desired length for the entire useful life of the product. Winner's Choice also has a patented method for serving strings (wrapping them in a material to prevent abrasion) that virtually eliminates serving separations.

Simple string maintenance is critical. This generally consists of nothing more than regularly waxing your string with a good wax such as Brownell's unscented string wax. Waxing the bowstring lubricates the fibers to prevent "fiber to fiber" abrasion, keeps the bundle of strands together, maintains and extends the life of the string, and prevents water absorption.

BOW LENGTH

Another important factor in selecting the right bow is the overall length. Generally speaking, bows with a shorter axle-to-axle length produce more raw arrow speed than longer bows. (The axle is the rod that holds the wheel at the end of the bow limb.)

Short bows with axle-to-axle lengths of between 33 and 38 inches are the most popular these days. In addition to being a bit faster than longer bows, shorter models work better with the mechanical aids most bowhunters now use in place of their fingers for releasing the arrow. Conversely, longer bows are better for fingers shooters because they reduce the amount of "finger pinch." Shorter bows are also easier to maneuver in the field, both among the limbs and branches encountered while you are hunting from a tree stand and when stalking through brush while you are hunting on the ground.

On the downside, shorter bows are more subject to the problems of hand torque (twisting) on the riser during the shot, which can result in poor accuracy. For that reason alone you don't want a bow that's much shorter than 34 inches unless you're an expert shooter.

STABILIZERS

Stabilizers are elongated metal bars that screw into the front of the riser. They help reduce hand torque of the bow handle at the shot, improving accuracy. They also help counterbalance the bow's rearward weight, offsetting its tendency to "jump" forward at the shot. The added weight of a stabilizer also facilitates your ability to steady the bow as you aim and release, and the stabilizer reduces vibration and noise during the shot.

They were once solid pieces of metal, but today the trend is toward hydraulic stabilizers, which improve performance. Generally speaking, the longer the stabilizer, the better it will work. Most hunting stabilizers are between 4 and 10 inches long. For many years I shot my bow without a stabilizer; however, I now use a relatively short (5-inch) hydraulic stabilizer. That's not because I like the extra weight or having a long rod sticking off the front of my bow, but because I can consistently shoot better with one.

OVERDRAWS

For years, a popular way bowhunters achieved more arrow speed was to use an overdraw. An overdraw is an arrow-rest bracket that extends 2 to 6 inches behind the riser, allowing you to shoot shorter, and therefore lighter, arrows. However, overdraws have their problems, the biggest being that they make it imperative for the archer to maintain excellent shooting form throughout the shot sequence to avoid torque, which would throw the shaft off-target. The longer the overdraw, the more exaggerated this problem can become.

I know several bowhunters who have shot an overdraw well for years, but I personally don't like them. They are an advantage for shooters with extremely long arms, though. For most of us, a better way to achieve a small overdraw effect is to use an arrow rest that bolts directly to the riser then "wraps around" the rear of the handle to produce, in effect, an overdraw about 1 inch long.

THE PERFECT HUNTING COMPOUND

You can read all the books and magazine articles and listen to an endless stream of advice, but the bottom line on choosing

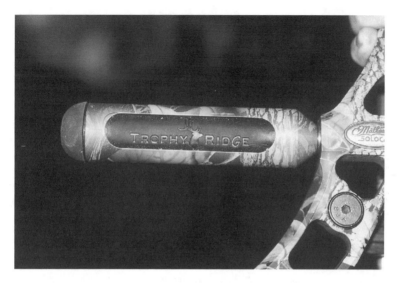

A stabilizer is a short to medium-length bar that screws into the front of the bow's riser to lessen hand torque, reduce vibration and noise, and help balance the bow. The best incorporate state-of-the-art vibration-damping materials.

the perfect hunting bow is this—you like it. It's a bow that simply feels good in your hand, looks good to you, and makes you happy to own it. It's set at the correct draw length for you, at a draw weight you can comfortably pull back, with a let-off you can hold for a reasonable length of time. To it you can attach modern accessories like a bow sight, quiver, and arrow rest. Virtually all major bow manufacturers build excellent hunting bows backed with a solid warranty, so the choice is yours.

The best place to buy your bow is from a reputable archery pro shop. Here you can "test drive" several different makes, models, and designs and get expert advice on the features and benefits of each along with accessories applicable to the kind of bowhunting you'll be doing.

Most important, the resident pro will help you set up your bow the right way, making sure the draw length and draw weight are correct, help you select the right arrow shafts, and

The two essential questions when choosing a new hunting bow are: Does it feel good to you? Can you shoot an accurate hunting arrow with it?

then help you tune your bow until it's shooting darts. He'll also be there when you have problems and need a little advice for working the kinks out of both your bow and your shooting form. Choosing a new bow in this manner can be time-consuming, not unlike shopping for a new car, but the end result will be a bow that you have confidence in, shoot well, and can enjoy for years.

THE MODERN ARROW REST

2

The differences between the basic bow-and-arrow setups used to shoot at game and targets just a decade or two ago and the hot-rod setups so popular today are astounding. In just fifty years the archery industry has evolved from a recurve bow, wood or aluminum shaft, glue-on broadhead, and finger tab or shooting glove to a short-axle compound bow, advanced aluminum or carbon or aluminum-carbon composite shaft, screw-in broadhead, and release aid. If you'd been asleep for twenty years and just woke up you'd have a hard time recognizing one of today's most popular bow-and-arrow setups.

Few archery items have evolved over the years as dramatically as the arrow rest, yet rests are often overlooked and underrated by archers more concerned with raw arrow speed and other accessory items that have more "sex appeal." Take it from me, using the wrong arrow rest is a formula for consistently poor shooting.

ARROW RESTS IN THE "OLD DAYS"

Archers with longbows did nothing more than rest the shaft across the fist of their bow hand, usually protecting against friction with a leather glove or sometimes nothing more than an adhesive bandage or strip of cloth tape. Next, in the 1950s, the then highly evolved recurve bow was designed with an arrow shelf carved into the grip. Archers covered these shelves with pieces of low-pile carpet, cloth, or leather and found that shooting "off the shelf" offered a big step up in consistent accuracy.

It wasn't until the 1960s that archers first began using removable arrow rests. These simply designed rests were usually little more than a horizontal plastic—or hair or feather—shelf for the arrow to rest upon and a plastic or nylon side plate for the shaft to rest against. Rests were soon developed that permitted some horizontal side-plate adjustments, which greatly aided in bowhunting and made accurate shooting at longer ranges a reality for skilled archers. Most of these rests attached to the bow with double-backed adhesive tape. These types of inexpensive arrow rests are still available today.

Arrow rests took a giant step forward in the mid-1960s with the introduction of the Berger Button. Invented by tournament shooter Norman Pint but named for well-known tournament shooter Victor Berger, this button cushioned the shaft against

The drop-away arrow rest has taken the bowhunting world by storm. That's because when the arrow rest launcher arm falls away at the shot, any possibility of fletch contact with the rest is eliminated, which is what you need for consistently accurate arrow flight.

side-to-side oscillation as it was released, which tightened arrow groups dramatically. It was often used in conjunction with the popular adhesive-backed Flipper or Flipper II arrow shelf, and this combination became the standard against which all other rests of the late 1960s and early 1970s were judged. Although you won't find any Berger Button/shelf rests today, you will find many similar arrow rests, now called by the generic name "cushion plungers."

A variation of the cushion plunger of the 1970s was the springy rest, which was nothing more than a threaded brass barrel connected to a coiled, one-piece, spring-wire plate-and-shelf unit. Springys were sold in a variety of spring gauges and tension weights to accommodate different bow weights and degrees of arrow stiffness and could be adjusted horizontally. These simple, rugged rests were popular with bowhunters of that era, but they're as rare as a four-leaf clover today.

In the 1980s we saw the rise in popularity of the prong, or launcher-type, arrow rests. These rest types were actually invented in 1967 by southern Californian Fred Troncoso, a professional musician and serious tournament archer who founded Golden Key–Futura a year later, making not arrow rests but the first rope release aids and a nock-aligner device. "I was shooting tournaments with Roy Huff, and he got me started making rests back then," Troncoso says. "I first just whittled rests out of wood and plastic. The first prong-type rest came about after I acquired my first Sable center-shot bow in 1967, which had a little wire rest, so I made a prong-style rest to fit this bow. This was before release aids were around, but it worked great anyway. But no one was really interested in them; they were too radical and complicated at the time."

Troncoso kept tinkering with his new rest design, "just trying to improve my own shooting," he says. "I just wanted to beat everyone else." Troncoso's first patented arrow rest was the Match One, patented in 1973–1974, followed by the Pace Setter Vee-launcher type rest a year later. "Even though my wife won three national field championships using the new rest, people still weren't that interested in such a new, radical design," Troncoso says. "After all, the arrow fell off if you turned the bow on its side! Sometimes it just takes a while for a good idea to catch on."

It wasn't until 1982–1983 that Troncoso's Vee-launcher rest first became accepted by a significant number of archers. Back then these rest types were commonly called wraparound rests because the rest unit attached to the Berger Button hole tapped into the off-side of the bow's riser, then "wrapped around" the back side of the riser. Initially there were two basic styles of this rest. The Vee-launcher type, like the old PSE Hunter Supreme and Martin Slide Rest, featured a solid metal post with a V-shaped cutout in which the arrow was rested. The Shoot-Through rest featured a pair of upthrust metal prongs, between which the shaft was rested. The Townsend Lodestar and PSE-CF-TM Hunter were two early examples.

The evolution of the arrow rest continues at a fast pace. Basic designs remain the same, but variations on the theme are widespread. Today's archer has more arrow rest makes, models, and designs to choose from than ever before. Such diversity is good, but it can also breed confusion. Which rest is the right one for you?

MODERN ARROW RESTS

Today arrow rests come in a seemingly endless array of styles and designs that, often as not, confound the novice. Common questions are, Why is rest category A better than category B? What features do I need on an arrow rest? Can I use the same rest for target shooting as I do for bowhunting?

Before choosing an arrow rest, you must have a basic understanding of how arrow shafts bend, or oscillate, when released. It may not appear so in real time, but high-speed photography has shown that arrows bend a surprising amount during the shot. The amount and type of bending are a direct result of shaft stiffness and the way the shaft was released. It is not until the shaft has traveled downrange that it recovers from this oscillation. Clearing the arrow rest at the shot is very important for accurate shooting.

Basically, when you release an arrow with your fingers, it oscillates from side to side as it leaves the bow, the first large bend away from the bow's handle. This type of release lends itself to the cushion plunger style of arrow rest, because as the shaft bends away from the bow it is bending away from the arrow rest too. Conversely, a shaft that has been released with a mechanical release aid tends to bend up and down, not side to side. This action lends itself better to the use of a Vee-launcher, prong-type, or drop-away arrow rest. That's because when the bowstring is released the first large bend the shaft takes is upward, away from the rest's two metal prongs.

"Our surveys indicate that somewhere between 80 percent and 90 percent of today's archers—and that includes both bowhunters and target shooters—use some type of release aid,"

Full-capture arrow rests like the Whisker Biscuit feature a bunch of stiff synthetic fibers set in a full circle with a hole in the center just large enough for the arrow shaft to fit through. The fibers hold the arrow securely in place until the shot, when the arrow and its fletching simply shoot right through with no real loss in accuracy, especially for bowhunters who shoot at whitetail deer at close range.

says Bob Mizek of New Archery Products, a leading manufacturer of arrow rests and broadheads. "That means that the basic
shoot-through rest design is the basic type of arrow rest that
most of them will be using. To that end, you're seeing a lot of the
industry's research and development efforts in the arrow rest
segment directed towards this type of rest."

FULL-CAPTURE RESTS

For years bowhunters using compound bows have had to deal
with their arrow shafts falling off their arrow rests, usually at
the worst possible time—like when a big buck or bull was standing broadside waiting to be shot. For a time they tried all sorts of
gimmicky gadgets that held the shaft in place until it was time
to shoot, but none of them were really very good.

Then along came a radical arrow rest design called the
Whisker Biscuit. The biscuit uses a bunch of stiff synthetic fibers
set in a full circle with a hole in the center just large enough for
the arrow shaft to fit in. The fibers hold the arrow securely in
place until the shot, when the arrow and its fletching simply
shoot right through the fibers with no real loss in accuracy, especially for bowhunters who shoot at whitetail deer at close range.

The Whisker Biscuit was an immediate success, so much so
that several other rest makers are now offering a variation on
the theme.

THE DROP-AWAY REST PHENOMENON

In 2003 I was at my local archery pro shop getting help setting
up a couple of new compound bows for the upcoming hunting
seasons. I asked the shop owner what he thought was the most
important accessory option over the last five years. "Drop-away
arrow rests," he said without hesitation. "It is the one thing I

recommend that every serious shooter and bowhunter add to his compound bow."

Muzzy Products Corporation introduced the first commerically successful drop-away rest, the Zero Effect, in 2001. Acceptance was slow, but once it picked up steam it was like a roller coaster. Here's why.

During the paper-tuning process it isn't unusual to find archers shooting bullet holes time after time with field points, but once broadheads are added to the equation the tears become imperfect. Hours later, after tweaking this and that, the paper tears remain inconsistent. On the target range, group size swells, especially at long range. Frustration sets in, confidence is shattered, and in the long run hunting success is negatively affected.

One of the big problems with this poor arrow flight has always been fletch clearance of the rest, though there are other variables at work as well, such as using the wrong arrow spine, problems with attaching the broadhead on straight due to minute bends in the ferrule or a bad shaft insert, or more commonly bad shooting form, usually a poor grip that creates torque at the shot. Fletch contact is why archers began using smaller vanes or feathers on their shafts—dropping from 5-inch to 4-inch fletches on aluminum shafts and to 4-inch, 3½-inch, or even 2½- to 3-inch fletches on carbon arrows. Smaller fletches have less chance of impacting the rest at the shot. This is also why the use of full helical fletching lost its glamour, with bowhunters more commonly using a slight helical or small 1- or 2-degree offset instead.

The trade-off is obvious. Smaller fletching cannot steer the shaft as well as larger fletching, especially when it is needed to help overcome the forward-steering propensity of broadhead blades. Fletching with less helical offset does not spin the shaft as rapidly, again reducing its ability to steer the shaft.

That's not to say that you cannot achieve superb arrow flight with broadheads using a prong-type rest. Of course you can. It is just that most bowhunters do not have the skills and/or patience to make the required minor adjustments, or the perfect shot-to-shot shooting form to remove torque from the equation. When you add the difficulties encountered in the field—weird body positions, awkward shooting angles, too many clothes in the way, a large dose of "buck fever"—unless everything is just so, the chances are that the arrow will not fly exactly as it is supposed to.

Enter the drop-away rest. Instead of using conventional prongs positioned to hold the shaft at roughly a 90-degree angle to the bowstring, with a drop-away rest the shaft is nocked and then laid on the riser shelf, usually in some sort of foam or plastic arrow holder. The rest's arrow launcher is positioned to the rear of, or slightly behind, the shelf and located below the arrow shaft, often not initially making any contact with the shaft. The launcher arm is attached to the bow's cable system with a rubber tube, cord, cable, or spring. When the bow is drawn, the downward cable movement sends the launcher upwards where it picks up the shaft and holds it in position at full draw. When the string is released, the rapid downward movement of the cable causes the launcher to "drop away" from the shaft. In essence, the arrow is streaking forward with no chance of making any further contact with the rest. The problem of fletch clearance has been solved.

The concept sounds simple, and it really is. Today several manufacturers offer a wide variety of drop-away rests. Just be aware that it takes a while to get a drop-away rest set up with your bow-and-arrow combination so that the shaft flies like a dart, which is why I recommend having them put on at your local pro shop. Once properly set up, they are relatively easy to tune and as reliable as the sunrise.

DESIRABLE DESIGN FEATURES

A look at the many different arrow rests currently offered for sale will turn up everything from the simple to the complex. Some rests have few adjustment features; others—notably those designed with the serious target archer in mind—have more screws and adjustment knobs than a rocket ship.

In recent years, the industry trend has been toward rests that can be micro-adjusted—that is, with vertical and horizontal adjustments that can be made in small increments. The goal is to permit precise vertical and horizontal rest adjustments so that an archer can perfectly tune his bow-and-arrow combination. However, many of these rests ultimately disappoint bowhunters, who find that their complex adjustment systems are difficult to work with and that the many tiny adjustment screws and knobs often rattle or slip during hunting season, which of course changes a shaft's point of impact.

Fortunately, the pendulum seems to be swinging away from complex and back to simple. Manufacturers have learned that bowhunters—their bread-and-butter customer base—want simpler designs that require less maintenance during the course of a hunting season.

"We feel that basic arrow rest design is returning to a more simplistic style," says Bob Mizek. "Our conversations with our bowhunting customers show that they want, first and foremost, reliability in their arrow rests. Second, they need to be able to make both vertical and horizontal adjustments easily, but then once they have been made, not worry about it again. They want simplicity without giving up the features. We know we can make everything super adjustable, but the reality is that often you end up with a bow-and-arrow setup that, once it's tuned and the arrow rest set, you never use the adjustment features of the rest again. We're trying to make rests simple to set up, quick to dial in, and built so they won't get beat up during tough field use and will hold up in extreme weather conditions."

ARROW REST COSTS

"While there are several price categories of arrow rests, we believe that today's archer who's not a beginner won't get sticker shock if a quality arrow rest falls into that $45–$60 price range," says Mizek. "Beginners may buy something a bit cheaper, but much higher than that you'll find some resistance. However, top-quality drop-away rests can cost upwards of a hundred bucks. We have found that the serious bowhunter of today is willing to pay that much for a top-quality drop-away rest that will help him shoot the most accurate broadhead-tipped arrow he can."

EFFECTIVE AIMING SYSTEMS

3

Few things in life get my goat more than poorly designed and cheaply made hunting accessories. And over the years few things have disappointed me more than one of the many different bow sights I've purchased and taken into the hunting woods. Lousy bow sights have cost me more than one opportunity at game. That's why I made myself a promise years ago—no fragile bow sights will ever find themselves attached to my riser again!

Fortunately for bowhunters, there are more excellent hunting bow sights available at reasonable prices today than ever before. Bow-sight design and manufacture are evolving rapidly, the result being that innovations like easy-to-see sight pins and/or stadia wires, easily adjustable sights featuring fewer moving parts, and compact construction are becoming common. Accessory and sight companies such as Advanced Archery Products, Chek-It, Cobra, Fine-Line, Fisher, Keller, Saunders, Sight Master, Sonoran Bowhunting Products, Specialty Archery Products,

Sure-Loc, Timberline Archery, Toxonics, and Tru-Glo, among others, all make excellent hunting bow sights. Many large bow companies—Browning, Hoyt USA, Martin Archery, and PSE, to name a few—also offer excellent hunting sights.

SIGHTING SYSTEMS

A bow sight is part of a total sighting system that can include a peep sight or kisser button, as well as some add-on sight accessories such as small lights for illuminating the top sight pin in dim light.

While some compound shooters hunt without a peep sight, every year more and more are discovering its advantages. A peep forces you to keep your head erect and anchored consistently, presenting the same sight picture shot after shot. Today it is unusual to find a bowhunter who does not use a peep sight. That's simply because using a peep will make you a consistently more accurate bow shot.

A peep sight will help you shoot a more accurate arrow. Be sure to use it with as large an aperture as possible.

The key to using a peep sight for bowhunting is to make sure the aperture is as large as possible. This lets in the maximum amount of light, critical when you're trying to find your pins or stadia wire at dawn or dusk. This large hole won't noticeably affect hunting accuracy. In the "old days," I used to take a Fine-Line Zero Peep Sight and use a quarter-inch bit to drill out the aperture hole as much as possible. Now most peep sight makers offer a full line of peeps featuring different-sized aperture holes for target shooting and bowhunting. Some peeps, like the Fine-Line Pick-A-Peep, come with adjustable apertures to make this process easier. Game Tracker's popular Dusk Vision Peep Sight uses four small neon polycarbonate fibers that gather light, which helps illuminate the viewing window in low-light conditions. The Shurz-A-Peep, Golden Key Line-O-Peep, and Pete Shepley Peep Sight are excellent peeps as well.

There are four basic bow sight types: fixed pin, movable pin, crosshair, and pendulum. Each has advantages and disadvantages, and each has a place in a bowhunter's repertoire under certain circumstances.

FIXED-PIN SIGHTS

By far the most popular sight type today, fixed-pin sights offer tremendous flexibility in that several sight pins can be added or removed as your needs dictate. Each of the pins can be set for a precise distance, and shots taken when not at these distances— as most shots at animals are—are sighted at "between the pins." Easily switching between pins set at different distances is also a big advantage when game is moving, allowing the hunter to track the animal and change pins instantaneously. Because of the simple design of most fixed-pin sights, they can be made with few moving parts and constructed like a rock.

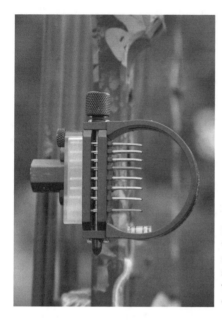

Fixed-pin bow sights are the most versatile and popular design in use today. Those with fiber-optic sight pins and a bubble level, like this Sonoran Hunter, are the best choice for most hunting situations.

The choices between the sight pins themselves are varied. Small-diameter pins are best when distances are long and light is good; larger-diameter pins are better in lower light. For many years the only pins available were 6/32 or 8/32 inch in diameter, but now some sights, like the Sonoran Hunter, feature thin, 0.026-inch wire pins.

The first sight pins designed to help bowhunters see in dim light, such as the Saunders T-Dot and Dot Sight Pin as well as the Meprolight Tritium sight pin, are fast being replaced by the new wave of fiber-optic sight pins. These pins use a colored polycarbonate fiber strand that gathers the maximum amount of available light in dim conditions when deer and other big game animals are most active, transferring it along the length of the fiber strand until it brightly concentrates in the fiber tip. This makes shots possible earlier and later in the day than ever before without the use of electronic lights. Almost all hunting sight companies now build their sights using some sort of fiber-optic sight pin material, for good reason: They are the smart choice for bowhunters expecting their best shot opportunities near dawn or dusk.

Also available today are various lighted sight pins. They are not legal in all states, but provide excellent low-light visibility. Many sight companies offer a light option on one or more of their hunting-sight models. Add-on lights also can be taped onto the bow riser or sight bracket to illuminate your pins. Just be sure to check state and local hunting regulations before using one.

CROSSHAIR SIGHTS

Though excellent for bowhunting, crosshair sights have waned in popularity in recent years. They function the same way pin sights do, with horizontal stadia wires moving up or down to place the arrow on target at a specific distance. Their vertical stadia wire helps keep the shooter from inadvertently letting the bow cant left or right during the shot, and also helps when shooting between the pins.

When crosshair sights first appeared, many were flimsy and broke easily. The best, however, are built to take the inevitable bumps and bruises a bowhunter will give them. Another disadvantage to early crosshair sights was their deep black stadia wires, which are almost impossible to see in critical low-light situations, especially when using a peep sight. Many bowhunters paint the stadia with fluorescent paint to overcome this handicap.

MOVABLE-PIN SIGHTS

The theory behind bow sights with movable pins is that by moving the single sight pin to adjust to the target distance, the archer could always aim with his pin dead on the target, thus eliminating the guesswork of shooting between the pins. The ideal situation would permit the archer to dial in the distance to the target with a range finder before coming to full draw.

Movable-pin sights have their proponents. Some open-country western bowhunters—where shots can range from in your face to way out there—depend on the combination of a laser range finder and a movable-pin sight to help them make precise shots at all distances. Some tree-stand whitetail hunters like these sights, too, setting their sight pin for a different specific distance when they change tree-stand locations.

The downside to movable-pin sights is revealed when the animal is moving, or appears suddenly out of the brush, and the distance is not known. Then the bowhunter is forced to guess the distance, and would probably be better served with a fixed-pin or crosshair sight. However, movable-pin sights do have a place in some bowhunting situations. I've used a Trophy Ridge movable sight a fair amount and have found that it works very well. Martin Archery also makes quality sights of this type.

PENDULUM SIGHTS

If ever a bow sight was designed for the tree-stand hunter, it is the pendulum sight. Here a single horizontal cross wire or pin is permitted to freely pivot on a hinge so that it rises as you take aim closer to the base of your tree and drops as you aim farther away. Together with a fixed vertical stadia wire, the two give a precise aiming point out to 30 to 35 yards, the exact distance being directly proportional to arrow speed. Beyond that distance the system breaks down. Some pendulum sights attack this problem by adding a couple of fixed horizontal pins or stadia wires to give the shooter an aiming point at longer distances.

The better pendulum sights allow you to adjust the length of the pivoting arm, thereby fine-tuning the sight for your individual bow's arrow speed. However, sights without this feature give acceptable accuracy at the distances for which they are designed to be used. One disadvantage of some pendulum sights is that they tend to be a bit noisy, and their moving parts can break or stick.

You'll find that tree-stand bowhunters who use pendulum sights would rather, as the old commercial used to say, fight than switch. There are several good pendulum sights on the market, including those by Keller, Saunders, and Advanced Archery Products.

IMPORTANT HUNTING SIGHT FEATURES

When it comes to hunting bow sights, the KISS principal—Keep It Simple, Stupid—applies. Bow sights with the fewest movable parts, that have the least number of screws and knobs, that need the fewest number of different Allen head wrenches to adjust and secure, and that are compact and relatively lightweight will cause you the least grief over time.

The better sights have simple vertical and horizontal adjustments. Many of today's sights also permit the entire sight pin block to be moved as a single entity while maintaining the solid integrity of the sight. This is a great feature, especially if you sight the bow in, then bump the sight bracket or find the bow goes out of tune just a bit and are forced to adjust the arrow rest or move the nock point slightly to regain the tune you want. You then must resight in only one pin, usually a midrange pin. The others are going to be very close to exactly on the money. This will save you a bundle of time.

One often-overlooked hunting sight feature is a rugged pin or stadia wire guard. A pin guard cannot be too beefy. After dinging pins for many years, I have often cannibalized a bow sight I didn't particularly like just to get its oversized pin guard for one I did like to shoot.

"I can remember back in the old days hunting with an old Merrill pin sight," says Jim Velasquez, president of bow quiver maker Sagittarius, a former tournament shooter, and an experienced bowhunter. "Once I was chasing a big bull elk and fell, totally trashing all my sight pins to the point I couldn't hunt any more. Ever since then I've believed that without a good pin guard a bow sight was useless for hunting." Some bow sights feature a beefy clear plastic pin guard that does two things—protects the fiber-optic sight pins and allows in more light for easier aiming in low-light situations.

Two other sight accessories have become popular in recent years. One is the addition of a small bubble level to the sight pin bracket, usually located at the bottom. The level allows you to know with a quick glance whether or not your bow is canted to one side or the other, which can cause your arrow to impact left or right of the target. Another popular addition is the use of a round sight pin guard in place of the old square pin guard. The theory here is that when looking at the sight through your round peep sight hole, mating the peep sight hole over the round pin guard will help you anchor your bowstring in exactly the same spot every time. Doing so is important to consistent accuracy, one reason this type of pin guard is so popular.

Hunting sights must also attach securely to the bow's riser. Some attach directly to the riser with two large screws; many more use a dovetail mounting system. The dovetail system provides the most flexibility while still holding the sight in place like cement. With a dovetail mount, you can easily remove the bow sight for transportation and then reattach it quickly and easily. One helpful hint is to use white paint or an indelible marker to mark the edge of both the male dovetail and female dovetail bracket with the sight attached. This way you can be sure that the sight is replaced in precisely the same position every time, assuring a consistent point of impact. To minimize noise I like to pad both the riser and the bottom of my sight's dovetail bracket with a small piece of stick-on felt before bolting the bracket down.

CHOOSING A HUNTING SIGHT

There's no secret formula in choosing a hunting bow sight except to select one that fits your shooting style, hunting technique, and personal preferences. With sight design and technology changing rapidly, the best way to see what's out there is to visit a well-stocked archery pro shop and look over several different makes, models, and designs. Ask the shop owner to let you shoot a couple of different sights on the indoor range. If two or three appeal to you about the same, make your decision based on the KISS principle.

However, KISS doesn't include the word "cheap." To avoid heartbreak at the wrong time—like when a good buck finally walks into range after a season of searching—buy the best sight you can afford. Then take your time and precisely adjust the pins or crosshair stadia wires until you know exactly where your bow is shooting at various distances. Doing so will help you enjoy shooting your bow and will increase your chances of success in the hunting woods.

ARROW SHAFT SELECTION

4

Bowhunters love to talk about their "stuff" and spend countless hours debating the merits of this arrow rest versus that, the advantages of bow sight A versus sight B, and so on. Yet when it's all said and done, the object of the entire exercise is to place a broadhead-tipped arrow shaft into the vitals of your quarry. Central to that task is a perfectly straight, correctly spined arrow that will fly with dartlike precision from your bow despite the attempts of a broadhead to steer it off course.

Fortunately for bowhunters, there are now more top-quality arrow shafts and shaft components from which to choose than at any time in history. Getting a shaft to fly straight and true with a broadhead attached has never been easier.

BASIC SHAFT COMPONENTS

A modern arrow shaft is made up of several components: the shaft itself, nock, fletching, and arrow tip insert. To build a shaft that will fly straight and true, each component must be made to work in perfect harmony with the others.

Although some traditional bowhunters continue to shoot arrows made of select wood, more than 95 percent of today's archers use arrows made from aluminum, carbon, or a combination of the two. We'll talk more about materials later in this chapter, but one thing you need to remember about arrow shafts is that they must be as straight as possible to fly true. Shaft makers will guarantee their shafts to be straight up to a certain tolerance, usually between ±0.004 and 0.001 inch. I've found that to fly perfectly straight with broadheads attached, shafts must have a straightness of at least ±0.002 inch.

When selecting a shaft for bowhunting, you must choose one with the correct "spine." High-speed photography has shown that shafts bend tremendously when shot from a bow. Spine refers to the amount the shaft will bend during the shot. Shafts of the proper spine will bend less and recover from this initial bending more quickly than those of improper spine, which results in more accurate arrow flight. The correct spine for your own bow is a function of several things, including your bow's draw weight and eccentric (wheel) design, your draw length, the arrow point weight, the type of arrow release you use (fingers or a mechanical release aid), and the shaft material itself. Fortunately, all shaft manufacturers produce shaft selection charts, which simplify the selection process.

Adequate fletching is critical in steering your shaft on a straight course. It is the job of the fletching to overcome the tendency of a broadhead's blades to try to steer the arrow, a formidable task. There are two basic fletch materials to choose from: natural feathers or plastic vanes. Feathers are softer and therefore more forgiving of any slight contact they might have with the arrow rest or riser during the shot. They also weigh less and are a bit faster than vanes. However, vanes are much tougher and are impervious to water and other climatic changes that can severely hamper the performance of feathers. For these reasons vanes dominate the market.

Most shafts today use three vanes glued to the shaft in a slightly helical, or offset, pattern. This encourages the arrow to spin like a perfectly spiraling football pass, not like a wobbling knuckleball. Most aluminum arrows are fletched with 4- to 5-inch-long vanes or feathers, while smaller-diameter carbon shafts generally are fletched with 2 1/2- to 4-inch vanes or feathers. On rare occasions, four vanes or feathers are used.

There are two ways to attach nocks and arrow points to an arrow shaft. The first is by "swaging," or gluing, them on. One or both ends of an arrow shaft are tapered to a solid point, over which a nock or an arrow point is then glued. Swaging was popular with traditional archers, but few bowhunters follow this practice today. Instead, modern archers use adapters that permit broadheads and target points to be screwed into the shaft, and tunable nock systems.

Aluminum screw-in arrow point adapters fit snugly into the hollow core of the shaft, where they are glued in. They are convenient, they are easy to use, and they make changing target points and broadheads quick and easy. They do add a small bit of weight to the overall shaft, but not enough to worry about. The key to using them properly is to make sure they are glued into the shaft as straight as can be.

Tunable nock systems are a million times better than the old glue-on nocks, and are one of the great advances in modern arrow shafts. Why? To achieve dartlike arrow flight, it is important that minimal—and preferably, no—contact be made between the fletching at the arrow rest or bow riser during the release. This is achieved by positioning the nocks so that the fletching clears these two obstacles.

Once the nock is glued on, that's it; the fletching is going where it's going, regardless. With a tunable nock—one that can be turned, or pivoted—the nock can be adjusted slightly to ensure perfect fletch clearance. This is a time-saving and convenient function, especially when you are tuning a bow or changing arrow rests or your style of release.

Arrow shaft components are little things, yet without the right components properly matched and attached to a shaft of the correct spine, you have been defeated before the battle has ever begun.

DOUG EASTON: ARROW SHAFT PIONEER

A discussion about modern arrow shafts would not be complete without mention of arrow shaft pioneer Doug Easton, whose arrows helped make shooting a bow popular for the masses of people who did not have time to mess with the intricacies of wooden shafts.

In 1922 Easton was a resident of the San Francisco Bay area and an avid archer and bowhunter who built his own first hunting bows and arrows in his teens. He experimented extensively with wooden arrow shafts, and many top competitive archers set records using his cedar arrows. In 1932 he moved his arrow-building business to Los Angeles, where he grew frustrated with the lack of consistency and uniformity between each piece of wood. He began to experiment with other shaft materials, and after extensive testing and research, produced the first Easton aluminum shafts in 1939.

After World War II Easton's production of aluminum arrows shifted into high gear. Easton developed a process of drawing 1-inch aluminum tubing down to the desired shaft size and continued improving shaft quality using thermal processes. These then-innovative production techniques led to the first aluminum arrow, the 24SRT-X. By 1948 Easton was producing 16 stock sizes of aluminum arrows.

In the early 1950s Easton developed the now-standard system of labeling aluminum arrow shaft sizes, in which the first two numbers represent the shaft diameter in sixty-fourths of an inch and the second two numbers indicate the shaft wall thickness in thousandths of an inch. (A 2413, for example, has a diameter of 24/64 inch and a shaft wall thickness of 0.013 inch.) In 1958, Easton developed the XX75 shaft, which was available in 22 different sizes. The company continued to grow, and eventually moved to a new plant in Van Nuys, California, in the late 1960s.

With Doug Easton's passing in December 1972, his son, Jim, took over as company president, and under his direction the company continued to explore the use of new materials and manufacturing processes to develop the next generation of arrow shafts. In the mid-1980s Easton expanded its operation to include a modern manufacturing facility in Salt Lake City, Utah, which today houses one of the largest aluminum anodizing operations in the country.

New products continued to come from the Salt Lake City facility. In the early 1980s Easton introduced the then-radical concept of wrapping a thin-walled aluminum core with layers of lightweight, high-strength carbon fiber. The result wan an extremely strong, stiff, lightweight, and durable arrow shaft. By 1984 the first composite shaft was used by Olympic archers to capture gold and silver medals. This concept lives on today in the form of the A/C/C, A/C/E, and Hyper-Speed shafts. (Another version, the X10, accounted for all but two of the medals awarded at the 1996 Olympic Games.) And in 1991, the XX78 Super Slam aluminum arrow shaft system was introduced. It featured new camouflage patterns and processes, a new adjustable nock system, and new methods of drawing aluminum tubing to a thinner wall thickness with extreme consistency.

Today Easton's aluminum arrow shafts dominate this sector of the arrow market. "From a cost/value standpoint, aluminum is hard to beat," said former Easton president Peter Weaver. "For a very low cost you can get an arrow shaft that's very consistent in weight, in spine, is easy to build into an arrow shaft, easy to tune into a bow, and durable enough to be straightened. Aluminum arrows are a proven product, and they have darn good utility."

CARBON SHAFTS COMING ON

For decades, aluminum was without question the king of the hill when it came to arrow shaft material. At the time, few bowhunters thought that new shaft materials might someday challenge aluminum's dominance. However, today that has all changed. While thousands of bowhunters continue to shoot aluminum arrows, the market leaders are now arrows shafts made from carbon (graphite).

Easton discontinued marketing their P/C pure carbon shaft when they acquired carbon-arrow maker Beman in 1995. Today they continue to develop and aggressively promote the Beman line of carbon shafts, the ST Axis line of small-diameter carbon arrows, and their aluminum-carbon composite shaft line, the A/C/C.

"With the A/C/C, we're refining what we think is a superior use of materials, optimizing what you can get out of both aluminum and carbon," said Weaver. "When you take the hoop strength of an aluminum core, which gives a precise foundation for component fit and sizing, and reinforce it with carbon fiber, you're utilizing the carbon fiber in the best way possible."

Carbon shaft sales have grown exponentially because they can provide several performance advantages over aluminum shafts. One is raw arrow speed, achieved because carbon shafts of the same length and spine as comparable aluminum shafts weigh much less. Another is durability. Carbon shafts are just plain tough, able to withstand much more abuse than aluminum and aluminum-carbon composite arrows. With carbon, the shaft

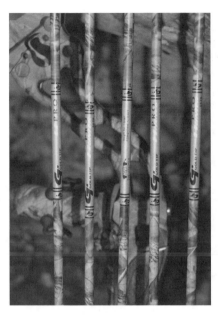

For many years aluminum arrow shafts dominated the market, but not anymore. While aluminum arrows are still popular, carbon arrows like these Gold Tip Pro Hunter shafts are now the choice of discriminating bowhunters due to their accuracy, durability, and deep penetration.

is either as straight as it was from the factory or it's broken—and it takes quite a wallop to break them. When aluminum is involved, as is the case with the A/C/C, the shafts can bend, often imperceptibly, and these bends can destroy accuracy. Carbon shafts also penetrate better than any other shaft on the market. Although there is no empirical, scientific research to back up this claim, there's no question in my mind that this is a fact.

While it took some time before archery pro shops jumped on the carbon arrow bandwagon, today finding a dealer who does not sell at least one major brand of carbon hunting arrow is virtually impossible "Using carbon shafts is a bit different than using aluminum arrows," says Jerry Fletcher, owner of Fletcher's Archery in Wasilla, Alaska, an experienced bowhunter and former Alaska state field archery champion. "For example, I've found that when tuning carbons, a 'perfect' paper tear isn't always the best in terms of the groups they'll shoot. Also, arrow rests that work well with aluminum arrows often don't work well with carbon shafts. And you sometimes need a bit more weight-forward

I weigh each and every one of my arrow shafts, as well as all my broadheads, prior to shooting them. My goal is to have a quiver full of finished arrows that weigh within 5 grains of each other. Such precision pays big dividends in consistent accuracy.

balance with a carbon shaft than you do with aluminum to get consistently tight arrow groups at longer yardages with broadheads." Fletcher recommends a weight-forward balance of between 12 and 18 percent with carbon shafts, whereas the standard for aluminum arrows is between 7 and 10 percent.

Several manufacturers currently offer pure carbon shafts for bowhunters, including Beman (owned by Easton), Blackhawk Archery, Carbon Impact, Carbon Tech, Game Tracker/AFC, Gold Tip, High Country Archery, and PSE Archery, among others.

CARBON SHAFT STYLES AND COMPONENTS

Early carbon shafts were so small in diameter that archers had to use an "outsert" to affix screw-on broadheads, field points, and nocks to them. Outserts are carbon components that glue over the shaft, creating a slightly larger diameter part than the rest of the shaft. This attachment system is still used by some manufacturers.

Early on, there was some trouble with attaching outserts to carbon shafts in a perfectly aligned manner. This, of course, adversely affected accuracy. Today, however, outserts are built to exact tolerances, and the bugaboos of attaching them to the shaft have largely been eliminated. If there is a downside to using outserts now, it is that a broadhead outsert requires the use of a shaft that is an inch longer than the arrow length would be if internal components were used. Failure to do this results in a shaft that, when drawn, will see the outsert skip over, and sometimes off, the arrow rest. Also, the overhang from the outsert often catches on the batting of a target, making it difficult to pull the shaft out of the target.

One of the downsides to some carbon shafts is the fact that they are so small in diameter, which means the fletching ends up being very close together where it is glued onto the shaft. When using popular prong- or launcher-type arrow rests, it is more difficult to achieve perfect fletch clearance with small-diameter shafts than with larger-diameter aluminum shafts. It takes careful tuning to avoid this problem.

Two companies—Gold Tip and Beman—began using internal components, á la aluminum shafts, in their pure carbon shafts in 1997. By 1999 virtually all other carbon shaft makers had followed suit. They could do so because the finished shafts are a bit larger in diameter than other carbon arrows. I began shooting these shaft types in 1997 and have been impressed with the way they perform. They fly like darts, they are consistent, and the larger diameter makes it easier to keep fletch contact off the prongs of my shoot-through arrow rest than with other, smaller-diameter carbon arrows.

As is the case with aluminum shafts, archers can use an adjustable nock system with all carbon shafts on today's market. This allows for a precise nock alignment regardless of the type of arrow rest you choose and makes it quick and easy to reset the nock position should you desire to change arrow rests.

FUTURE TRENDS

One trend among today's bowhunters is that more of them are shooting expensive shafts. Modern bowhunters want the best shafts they can shoot and are willing to pay for them. This is evident in the increased sales of carbon arrows over the past half-decade, with more and more bowhunters switching to carbon every year. Carbon shafts cost a few more dollars than aluminum arrows per dozen—top-of-the-line carbon arrows sell for nearly a hundred bucks a dozen retail—but discriminating bowhunters realize that in the overall scheme of what it costs to own top-quality archery equipment and go bowhunting, a few more dollars for arrow shafts is money well spent.

"One of the things we see in archery is an aging demographic. People in the sport are a bit older and have a little more money to spend on equipment," notes former Easton president Weaver. "They're definitely starting to move up the ladder in terms of arrow shafts. The guy who shot GameGetters 10 years ago is shooting XX75s and XX78s today, and in some cases A/C/Cs—3D archery has really helped promote them. More bowhunters have started shooting A/C/Cs than we initially thought would."

Going hand in hand with that trend is a shift to using shafts with tunable components, especially tunable nocks. Weaver's data shows the same thing. "I think we are getting a more knowledgeable group of archers out there," he says. "Maybe that's because we don't have as much influx of new archers as

When bowhunting dangerous game you cannot scrimp on your equipment. I shot this big Alaskan brown bear at 17 steps with a Gold Tip 7595 Pro Hunter carbon shaft tipped with a 125-grain Thunderhead broadhead. He only ran 20 yards before piling up.

we did years ago, which may be a problem for archery in general, but it is creating a more knowledgeable shooter as a percentage of the marketplace. These people appreciate the features of adjustable nocks, easily replaced components, a choice of different arrow shaft sizes, and so on."

So what's on the arrow shaft horizon? Only time will tell. But one thing's for certain—today's manufacturers are not standing still when it comes to shaft development.

"We continue to work on improving our aluminum shafts, but we're continually looking at anything and everything out there, stuff like boron, Kevlar, and so on," Weaver says. "Kevlar, for example, doesn't have any value by itself. It adds lots of strength and weight, but it doesn't have any stiffness. But that's the process. We look at all materials out there, all the resin systems, all the composites, thermoplastics, and so on. Nothing is sitting on the horizon right now that we're aware of that will appear tomorrow as the all-new, breakthrough new material. Where we've come with aluminum, aluminum-carbon composites, and pure carbon are really the only choices today that offer reasonable performance values to the consumer. But if we find something that will work better, you can be sure we'll use it."

BROADHEADS FOR BOWHUNTING

5

bowhunter heading into the deer woods to try and "make meat" these days has a wide variety of high-performance equipment available from which to create the optimum bow-and-arrow setup. But without a strong, razor-sharp broadhead that will surgically slice through an animal's vital organs, arteries, and veins—causing a quick, humane death—all the work, planning, and hope are for naught.

Fortunately, today's market offers a huge array of choices when it comes to quality broadheads for hunting deer and other big game. Understanding what's available and the advantages and disadvantages of each style and design is the first step in selecting the right broadhead. You should also keep in mind that, like other archery equipment, broadheads continue to evolve. Never overlook new developments, but at the same time assess them with a skeptical eye. Make sure that a new type or style of broadhead will do the job you need it to do before switching from a proven winner.

Here's a look at what's available.

FIXED-BLADE HEADS

Traditional broadheads have been cleanly killing deer and other big game since the days of primitive man. This system—in which two, three, or four nonreplaceable blades are attached to a center ferrule that is either glued on or screwed into the arrow shaft—can still be found in the deer woods each fall. These broadheads generally have a cutting-tip design and are relatively heavy, weighing between 140 and 175 grains, although some weigh as little as 125 grains and some as much as 220 grains.

Most bowhunters who currently use this type of broadhead are traditional shooters who hunt with recurves or longbows. However, there is a group of compound shooters who use this type of broadhead, too, believing that when deer hunting from a tree stand—where shots are typically less than 25 yards—a super-strong, deep-penetrating head that cuts a huge hole is more important than a lightweight head designed more for aerodynamics than strength.

REPLACEABLE-BLADE HEADS

The replaceable-blade head is the most popular basic style of broadhead found in the woods today. Like all good equipment, it has evolved over the years, the design changes mirroring the advances in efficiency found in modern hunting bows and arrow shafts.

When bowhunters shot slower recurve bows loaded with heavy arrow shafts, a large, heavy, two-bladed, cutting-tip type of broadhead with blades that had to be hand-sharpened made all the sense in the world. When compound bows came on the scene, an arrow speed of 220 feet per second was hot stuff. To match this increased speed, broadhead size dropped until the three-blade, 125-grain head became the most popular. With today's highly efficient compounds sending their shafts off at somewhere between

250 and 290 feet per second—some even faster—the most popular broadhead size, according to major manufacturers, has dropped to 100 grains.

The big advantage to replaceable-blade broadheads is that bowhunters don't have to hand-sharpen their own blades. Instead, they can quickly and easily replace used blades with inexpensive, fresh, scalpel-sharp blades in seconds. In fact, manufacturers recommend *against* the shooter sharpening these blades at all. Their tests show that the only thing you can do is dull them. The best replaceable-blade broadhead designs also incorporate secure locking systems that prevent the blades from coming loose on impact. They're just as dependable as the old-style fixed-blade broadheads ever were.

Replaceable-blade heads come in two basic styles—cutting tip and chisel point. Years ago, it was believed that the cutting-tip design, in which the head's sharp blades extend all the way to the broadhead's forward tip, penetrated better than the chisel point. The blades on chisel-point heads do not extend to the broadhead's forward tip, instead stopping a bit short of that mark. The nose consists of a piece of metal shaped like a chisel point, with some manufacturers sharpening the edges. Recent research has shown that the difference in penetration between the two designs is negligible.

MECHANICAL HEADS

The tendency of broadhead blades to act as airfoils that can steer an arrow wildly out of the bull's-eye is the big reason expandable-blade, or mechanical, broadheads have increased in popularity in recent years. Their development goes hand in hand with the proliferation of today's super-high-speed bows and lightweight arrow shafts with small fletching. This combination is more difficult to precisely tune with the large-diameter, fixed-blade and

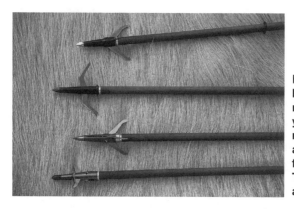

Mechanical broad-
heads are becoming
more popular each
year as companies
refine their designs
and improve manu-
facturing processes.
They are not legal in
all states, however.

replaceable-blade broadheads that have been a mainstay of bowhunting since its earliest days.

A mechanical broadhead features blades—usually two or
three, but sometimes more—that are connected to the ferrule by
a hinge system, which allows them to be folded forward into the
ferrule before the shot. Upon contact with an animal, the blades
are driven out and backward until they lock into the ferrule. The
blades are then in the same cutting position as those found on
fixed- and replaceable-blade broadheads, and thus perform the
same cutting function.

The advantages of this system are many. First, by removing
the airfoil of the fixed blades and creating a low-profile arrow tip,
these arrows fly almost identically to arrows with target tips of
the same weight. The superior aerodynamics of these heads were
designed to be used with high-speed compound bows pushing
small-diameter, lightweight arrow shafts—specifically carbon
and aluminum-carbon composite arrows—with small fletching
at 250 feet per second or more. Their low profile also makes a
bow/arrow/broadhead combination easier to precisely tune than
when using fixed-blade broadheads. Expandable broadheads also
achieve a wider cutting path through an animal than most other
heads of the same weight. The most popular fixed- and replaceable-
blade broadheads have a cutting diameter of between 1 and 1¼

inches, but most expandables start at 1½ inches, with the majority in the 1⅞- to 2½-inch range. In bowhunting, the bigger the hole, the better off you are.

My personal experience with mechanical heads has grown over the years. I have taken whitetails, black bears, and elk with them, all with excellent results, but my feelings on mechanical broadheads have remained unchanged over the last decade since they first appeared. I've found that most expandables tune and fly well, and I have had many glowing reports from friends who have used them when whitetail hunting. The large-diameter exit hole created by an expandable's ultrawide cutting surface is awesome and a definite advantage. However, there are poorly designed mechanical heads out there that can cause you grief when their blades fail to open on impact as advertised. Mechanical heads should not be used with bow-and-arrow setups that produce relatively low raw arrow speed because it takes speeds approaching 240 feet per second to ensure that you'll achieve adequate penetration and that the blades will open properly.

Today there is a new mechanical head design in which the blades are affixed to the broadhead ferrule by means of a replaceable cartridge. When the head strikes the target, instead of the blades folding back into the open position, the cartridge itself slides backward to expose the blades. This design offers two big advantages over the older style. First, because the blades slide backward they offer less resistance, which means they penetrate better. And second, the cartridges are replaceable, meaning you can practice with your broadheads, then pop in a fresh cartridge with scalpel-sharp blades before heading afield.

Before counting on using mechanical broadheads for bowhunting, be advised that some states have restrictions on the species that may be hunted with mechanical broadheads or simply do not allow them at all during big game hunting seasons. So, before deciding that these sleek missile-like heads are the cat's meow, check the regulations to make sure they're legal where you hunt.

WHAT TO LOOK FOR

Regardless of the style and type of broadhead you select for hunting, there are several factors to consider. Foremost is quality construction. Manufacturers who spend the extra few bucks to make sure that their manufacturing tolerances are tight and only use high-quality materials produce broadheads that are consistent shooters and hold together on impact. This is not the case with all broadheads. For example, I once weighed six-dozen identical broadheads from a popular manufacturer to see how close they actually were to the advertised 125 grains. To my surprise, almost all weighed between 130 and 135 grains, with some weighing as much as 140 grains. This kind of inconsistency will result in inconsistent arrow flight and make tight arrow groups impossible to achieve. Yet to read this manufacturer's advertising, you'd think they were carefully making high-performance rocket ships with the latest high-tech, space-age materials.

Some manufacturers do cut corners, but the smart ones know that serious bowhunters are willing to spend a few more dollars for top-quality broadheads. When Barrie Archery, a company with a long track record of producing excellent broadheads, introduced a 100-grain, replaceable-blade head with a titanium ferrule that cost nearly $10 apiece at retail, the skeptics howled that they'd never sell enough to make ends meet. Yet Barrie couldn't make them fast enough and soon expanded the titanium line to include additional weight sizes of 85 and 125 grains.

When shopping at your local archery pro shop, ask to examine the new broadheads you are considering. Take them out of the package and check them for quality construction. Assemble the heads, screw them into an arrow shaft, and give them the spin test, spinning them rapidly on their tip and checking for the telltale wobble that can indicate a bent ferrule. Make sure that all the components—specifically the blades, blade-locking collar, and ferrule—mate tightly together. Ask to weigh them on the shop's grain scale.

Next, use a broadhead that flies well with your chosen bow-and-arrow setup. I have found from time to time that a particular broadhead make and model just would not tune perfectly with my bow unless I made adjustments to the bow itself—changing the draw weight, shortening the draw length, changing arrow rests—that I wasn't happy making. When that happens, it's time to move on to a different broadhead.

One of the problems with some modern archers is that, in the search for the fastest possible bow-and-arrow setup they can shoot, they are going to lighter and lighter broadheads. Sometimes they'll choose heads that weigh as little as 75 grains. This isn't necessarily bad, except when the ultralight broadhead does not provide enough front-of-center (FOC) balance to the arrow shaft.

Without the proper FOC balance, the shaft will not fly perfectly. Front-of-center means that rather than balancing at the shaft's midpoint, the arrow should instead balance a bit forward of that point. To determine FOC balance, measure your overall arrow length with the broadhead attached. If the length is 30 inches, your midpoint is 15 inches. Mark this spot on the shaft with a felt pen. Now move one finger forward under the shaft until the arrow balances perfectly on your fingertip. This is your balance point. Mark this spot with the felt pen. The ideal FOC balance on an aluminum hunting arrow shaft is generally somewhere between 7 and 10 percent of the arrow length—in this case, a balance point somewhere between 2 and 3 inches forward of the shaft's center point. With some lightweight carbon shafts, a bit more exaggerated FOC of between 12 and 18 percent can produce better arrow flight.

Never hunt with broadheads unless the blades are so sharp they scare you. Dull blades will not slice cleanly through arteries and veins, the kinds of cuts that bleed freely and are slow to clot. We owe it to the game we hunt to try and kill them as quickly and humanely as possible. Razor-sharp broadhead blades are the only ones that can get the job done.

The last consideration in selecting a broadhead for bowhunting should be price. Too many bowhunters try to save a dollar or two when purchasing broadheads, when in reality the broadhead is the one piece of bowhunting tackle that should never be compromised. At the moment of truth, the last thing you need to worry about is whether or not your broadhead will fly straight and true, penetrate deeply, and hold together should it inadvertently strike a leg or shoulder bone.

There are now more quality broadheads from which to choose than ever before. The relatively new mechanical broadheads are growing in popularity, but they are still in their infancy and are not the right choice for everyone. The key to both success and satisfaction lies in carefully selecting the right broadhead design, style, and size to match both your current bow-and-arrow setup and the conditions under which you'll be hunting.

SHOOTING ACCESSORIES

6

You'll need several accessory items to complete your bow-shooting system. These smallish pieces of equipment may not look like much at first, but once you've been shooting your bow a while, and have been on a few bowhunting trips, their importance will not seem trivial. Here are several accessories you'll want to consider.

FINGER TABS, RELEASE AIDS

A fundamental decision you'll have to make is whether to release your bow with your fingers or with a mechanical release aid of some sort. (We'll talk more about each style in Chapter 8.) Regardless of the style you choose, you'll need accessory items to help you.

If you're a fingers shooter, you'll need a finger tab or shooting glove to protect your fingers from the abrasive bowstring. At one time leather shooting gloves were the cat's meow for fingers shooters, and they are still popular with some traditional archers. Most compound shooters use a finger tab, which is held in place by a plastic ring that fits over the middle finger and can be slipped over bare fingers or gloves. Tabs can be rotated over the back of the hand, freeing your fingers for other work, then quickly rotated into place when it's time to shoot.

Most tabs slide off the string with a facing of calf's hair, leather, or plastic. All work well. I personally like the calf's hair tabs best, even though they wear out and have to be replaced from time to time. Plastic and leather tabs wear longer and work very well, too. Most tabs also come with a thick plastic finger spacer to prevent you from pinching the arrow shaft between your fingers when you draw and shoot, something that can adversely affect arrow flight. Make sure any tab you buy has this spacer.

Archery industry estimates show that between 80 and 90 percent of modern bowhunters release their arrows with some type of mechanical release aid instead of with their fingers. The reason is simple: A release makes it easier to shoot a consistently accurate arrow. This fact was first demonstrated more than a quarter-century ago, when simple releases started replacing finger gloves on the competitive target circuit. As release design evolved and manufacturing techniques improved, quality releases became readily available and affordable. Today archers can choose from myriad designs and styles in prices ranging from a few bucks to over a C-note.

How does the mechanical release produce more accurate arrow flight than a finger release? Simply stated, when you grip the bowstring at a single point, as you do with a mechanical release, you achieve a more consistent release than you do with a finger tab or shooting glove sliding off the same string. Also, arrows shot with a release tend to flex and vibrate less at the shot, which makes the bow easier to tune properly, especially with broadheads. And since these arrows bend less, you can tune the

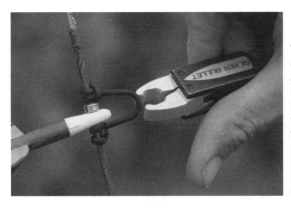

The wrist-strap, caliper-style release aid, like this Pro Release Silver Bullet, is the most popular with bowhunters these days. When paired with a string loop, it is hard to find a more consistently accurate combination.

bow with a lighter arrow shaft than you could with the same setup using fingers. This translates into higher raw arrow speed and flatter trajectory, making distance estimation less critical.

Three more factors stand out among the reasons for the increase in release-aid popularity. First, in today's go-go world, our discretionary time has shrunk. People simply have less time to tune and practice shooting their bows. By using a quality release aid, these archers can learn to shoot more accurately much faster than they can with fingers. Second, as bow manufacturers continue their quest for high-speed, energy-efficient bows, more quality bows are built with a short axle-to-axle length. This design favors the use of a release over fingers. And third, manufacturers continue to improve their products, offering the consumer an annual wave of new high-quality release aids in a variety of designs over a wide spectrum of prices.

Most release aids grab the bowstring with either a set of metal caliper jaws or a rope. Although there are several variations on the theme, these releases can be defined by the way they are triggered. In this there are three basic designs: index finger–triggered, thumb-triggered, and back-tension-triggered. (Back-tension releases are triggered by contracting the back muscles, not by a trigger hit with the index finger or thumb.) The basic caliper-type, index finger–triggered release has dominated the market for years. Most shooters using this type of release choose one with some sort of wrist strap, which makes smoothly drawing the bow using the back muscles easier than when using a release without the strap.

"The index finger–trigger-fired caliper release is the most popular design by far," says Gary Todd of Pro Release, a leading release-aid manufacturer. "They have about 85 percent of the bowhunting market. For bowhunting, the caliper-type releases with either a single or double jaws really dominate things. The rope releases and what I call 'therapeutic releases,' like the back-tension releases that help guys with target panic, are really more popular with target shooters. Generally speaking, beginning bowhunters should stay away from these styles."

One reason caliper-type releases are the most common is the increasing popularity of using a "string loop" on the bowstring. A string loop is a short piece of small-diameter cord tied in a loop over the nock point of the bowstring. Instead of the release grabbing the string itself, it grabs this loop. This distributes the pressure of the release equally above and below the arrow nock, which facilitates the arrow leaving the bowstring perfectly level and consistently shot after shot. The loop also eliminates wear on the bowstring's serving, caused by contact with the release aid's metal jaws.

Both archery pro shop owners and manufacturers say that while most archers are price conscious when it comes to purchasing a new release aid, trying to save an extra few bucks on a release can lead to poor accuracy and long-term disappointment. "There are some releases out there built from inexpensive imported parts and powdered metal using questionable machining practices," says Todd. "In order for a release aid to function properly, you have to hold machining tolerances to a hundredth of an inch or less. Many of these cheaper products do not, yet they are touted as low-cost alternatives to more expensive models. In the long run these cheapie releases will disappoint the consumer. A quality hunting release is moderately priced, in the $35–$75 range. Bowhunters should stay away from bottom-of-the-barrel releases."

The best way to start shooting a release is to visit your local archery pro shop. There you can play with several different models and designs, get expert advice, and shoot a few arrows on the shop's indoor lanes to get a feel for each. The pro shop can also help you set up your bow and help you tune it using a release. (Bows must be retuned and resighted in when switching from a finger release to the use of a mechanical release aid, and vice versa.)

A mechanical release aid may not be Robin Hood pure, but using one *is* the best way to achieve consistently accurate arrow flight.

ARM GUARDS

An arm guard may not seem like much, but it is one of the most important accessory items a bowhunter can use. Arm guards are designed to keep the bowstring from "slapping" the inside forearm of your bow arm when you release the arrow. This is a common problem with beginning shooters, but rarely happens to those who have some experience. The big value of an arm guard in bowhunting is not protecting your arm, but protecting the bowstring itself.

How so? In cool or cold weather, you'll be wearing thick, heavy clothes. The oversized or baggy sleeves of a heavy shirt or jacket can inadvertently catch your bowstring at the shot, causing your arrow to be launched like a drunken duck. That's why a bowhunter needs an arm guard. It doesn't have to be fancy or expensive. Most arm guards cover the inside of the forearm, have a Polarfleece or slick face, and are attached to the arm with three or four stretch strings and Velcro. You can get a good one for under $5.

QUIVERS

Quivers are used to store, protect, and transport your arrows to and from the field. All quivers feature a hood to hold and protect your broadheads, and a series of arrow shaft grippers to hold the lower end of the shafts. There are two basic types: quivers that attach to the bow and non-bow-attached quivers that are carried on the archer's hip or back.

There is a small debate about which type of quiver is best for bowhunting. On one hand, a famous bowhunting personality swears that using a bow-attached quiver is a formula for disaster, causing excessive bow torque, an overbearing weight imbalance, and missed shots at game. On the other hand, bow-attached quiver makers swear this isn't so. Because there's been no definitive, scientifically valid way to prove or disprove either theory, the controversy rages on.

What's the answer?

"If you ask the question, does a bow-attached quiver affect accuracy, yes or no, the answer would have to be 'yes,'" says Randy Ulmer, a several time 3-D and field shooting world champion, as well as a highly accomplished bowhunter. "But does it make any real difference in bowhunting? I'd have to say no, it does not."

Jim Velasquez, president of bow quiver maker Sagittarius, is a serious and accomplished bowhunter who has done some

Two-piece, bow-attached quivers are now the bowhunting norm. The best, like the Mathews Arrow Web, incorporate cutting-edge vibration-damping technology, which helps quiet them down to a whisper at the shot.

testing on this subject. He also believes a bow quiver's effects on hunting accuracy are minimal.

"Years ago, we made a shooting machine, because we wanted to see what the differences would be with and without a bow quiver and without human error affecting the shooting," Velasquez says. "We shot in excess of 400 arrows out to 40 yards, using four, six, and eight arrows in the quiver. We saw a very insignificant difference in point of impact in comparison with no quiver attached to the bow. When we went down from eight arrows to one arrow in the quiver, we did see a small, but very insignificant, point of impact change, but it wasn't enough to make any difference in a person's ability to hit a kill zone in hunting situations."

All quiver makers emphasize that if you hunt with a bow-attached quiver it is important that you tune your bow with the quiver attached and practice shooting that way, too. Tuning a bow without the quiver, then randomly attaching one the day before hunting season begins is a sure formula for inaccurate shooting. They also emphasize that all parts and screws must be tight, which will help dampen any noise produced at the shot.

One of the biggest advancements in bow quiver design has been the inclusion of vibration-damping materials in the quiver itself. In the old days, a bow quiver was one of the noisiest accessories added to a hunting bow. Then Mathews Archery, a leading maker of single-cam bows, included their patented harmonic damping system into their bow quivers, and vibration and noise were a thing of the past. Since then many other bow and quiver makers are adding some sort of vibration-damping material. It's a huge step forward.

RANGE FINDERS

The more you bow hunt, the more you'll realize that the number-one reason people miss shots at game is that they misjudge the distance to the target. Just how critical is accurate range estimation? Even from the fastest compound bow, an arrow shaft traveling 300 feet per second will drop more at 30 yards than a bullet from a .30-06 at 300 yards. With this same super-fast compound, if you misguess the distance to a deer-sized target standing broadside at 40 yards by ± 3 yards, you're going to miss the 8-inch-diameter heart/lung "kill zone," even if your shot was perfect.

For that reason, all bowhunters should practice estimating range with the naked eye. But this is not a bombproof method, and it breaks down even for the most skilled bowhunters out past 35 or 40 yards. This difficulty is what spurred the first range finders. At first all we had to use were "coincidence" range finders, popularized by Ranging, which use the triangulation principal. That is, they have two windows and a combination of prisms and lenses that produce two separate images the user sees when looking through the sighting window. As you view the object, you turn a dial with your finger until the images coincide and appear as one. You then read the distance on the dial. In skilled hands these range finders can be reasonably accurate.

Laser range finders have taken this to the next level. With the press of a button, these units send out a beam of light, which is reflected off the target object back to the unit. The unit measures the time it takes for this reflection to go out and back

The modern laser range finder is a superb bowhunting tool, allowing the archer to instantly know the exact distance to the target with the push of a single button.

to calculate the distance. Laser range finders are accurate to ±1 or 2 yards from distances as close as 10 yards or out to a half-mile or more, and you can get an accurate reading in less than a second.

Bushnell offered the first laser units for bowhunting, the Yardage Pro 400 and Yardage Pro Compact 600. Today many other companies, including Leupold, Leica, Swarovski, Nikon, and Simmons also make excellent units suitable for bowhunting. Some expensive units also include a binocular in combination with the range finder. Laser range finders are powered by AA or 9-volt batteries and cost somewhere between $300 and $1,200.

Range finders are usually used to take readings off stationary objects, not animals. They work best when calculating the exact distance to an object that you expect an animal to walk past. When it gets there, you don't have to guess where to hold your sights. You know. Such knowledge translates into more perfect hits, the goal of all bowhunters. For this reason I never head afield without a laser range finder.

TARGETS

Unless you do all your practice shooting at a local pro shop or outdoor range, you'll need at least one target for practice. There are several different types and designs.

For field-tip practice, the best choice is a bag-type target. These targets will last for thousands of shots and feature materials that make arrow removal easy, regardless of shaft material or arrow speed. Morrell, Delta (Deadstop series), Arrow Brake, and Southern Archery all make good ones.

The same bag-type targets you use for field-point practice won't work with broadheads. The most popular broadhead targets on the market today employ multiple layers of a Styrofoam material that has been tightly compressed. These targets can take hundreds of hits from even large-diameter broadheads before being shot out. The leader in this is Field Logic, makers of the Block line of targets. Others who make excellent targets of this type include Black Hole, Morrell, American Whitetail, and Tru-Glo.

Three-dimensional targets are extremely popular for bowhunting practice. They are replicas of big and small game animals, from deer to elk to bears to turkeys and a variety of small game. These targets are made from a high-density, self-healing foam and offer the best preseason shooting practice of all. McKenzie, Delta Targets, and Field Logic are the leaders in 3-D target manufacturing.

TUNING YOUR BOW 7

Bow tuning has become something of a mystery with present-day bowhunters. Some people make it out to be a process that only a magician can do. Others, turned off with the thought of dealing with the mechanics of their compound bows, don't even worry about it.

Tuning is the process of adjusting (with the proper arrow being used) the arrow rest, pressure point, string height, draw weight, and nocking height of the bow to achieve optimum arrow flight. Sounds difficult, doesn't it? In truth, tuning a modern compound bow isn't all that tough. Anyone with the right arrow shafts, bow accessories, and a few simple tools can do it. Why bother with bow tuning at all? Because only a well-tuned bow will produce consistent dartlike arrow flight, which in turn produces optimum accuracy and penetration of game—both critical to success in the field.

Let's face it: Most of us are bowhunters, not bow technicians. Although we enjoy shooting our bows, we'd rather be in the field, hunting, than in the shop tinkering with equipment. But we also know that getting into the in-your-face range needed for a good bow shot at game is tough. It doesn't happen every day. When we do get there, we want to make sure that our bows will deliver the accurate arrow necessary to close the deal. Without a well-tuned bow, the chances of that happening are slim. And that's not acceptable.

To tune your bow, you'll need a few basic tools. These include a bow square, nock pliers, and the various Allen wrenches necessary for adjusting your bow's limb bolts and the adjustment screws of your arrow rest. You'll also need a target butt to shoot into and a paper rack to shoot through. A bow scale, to measure the bow's exact draw weight, is helpful but not necessary.

Of course, you can always take your bow to your local archery shop, where the resident pro can help you tune your bow-and-arrow setup. He'll have all the right tools and will be able to assist you in getting everything in synch. I recommend that all novice archers take this route. In fact, most pro shops include initial bow tuning as part of the purchase price of a new bow. However, knowing how to tune your own bow is beneficial. It not only gives you a good idea of how everything works together to produce perfect arrow flight, but you'll then be able to periodically check your bow's tune during the course of the year, making small adjustments needed with a minimum of fuss and muss. You will also have the skills to make emergency field repairs when the nearest pro shop is either closed or too far away to be of practical help.

MATCHED EQUIPMENT

Unless you have the right arrow shafts of the correct length with the proper spine for your bow, tuning is impossible. The manufacturer's shaft selection chart is the place to find this information. You also need arrow points of the same weight. It should go without saying that your arrows should all be built the same, with identical fletching, nocks, and screw-in arrow point inserts. The goal here is to shoot arrow shafts that are both built from the same components and are as close to the same weight as possible.

You'll also want an arrow rest that is adjustable both in and out, and up and down. Rests with micro-adjustment features are the easiest to tune. Generally speaking, a shoot-through, or Vee-launcher, type of rest works best with a release aid, and a cushion plunger rest works best for fingers shooters. It's also important to have all your bowhunting accessories—including bow sight, peep sight, string silencers, bow quiver, and stabilizer—attached when you tune the bow.

STEP-BY-STEP BOW SETUP

To ready your new bow for tuning, do the following:

1. Check the tiller, making sure that both upper and lower limb tillers are the same. You can do this while adjusting the bow's draw weight to the setting you desire.

2. Make sure the bow is set at your exact draw length. If not, adjust it. (In most cases, you'll need a bow press to do this. If you don't have one, take the bow to the pro shop).

3. Attach the arrow rest, following the manufacturer's instructions. Then, adjust the rest's "center shot" (the left/right position of the rest) to a dead-on setting. To do this, nock an arrow and place it on the rest. Holding the bow at arm's length, use the bowstring as a reference point while looking at the tip of the shaft. This should be hidden by the bowstring. If it sticks out from the string, move the rest back in. If it's in toward the bow handle, move the rest back out.

4. Using the bow square, place a nock set on the bowstring. The bow square will allow you to place the nock set precisely. Start

with the nock set 1/4 inch above center and, using your nock pliers, crimp it down medium-hard. You may have to move it later, but this should get you close.

5. Attach your bow sight, peep sight, stabilizer, string silencers, and quiver to the bow, following the manufacturer's instructions.

6. Turn your arrow nocks. This means turning the nock so that the fletching will not contact either the arrow rest or bow riser during the shot. You can do this visually by placing a shaft on the string, setting the shaft on the rest, and eyeballing the fletching from the rear to find obvious contact points. A good test for fletch contact is to spray a fine white powder (foot powder works well) onto the arrow rest and riser, then shoot an arrow. Check the riser and rest for places where the arrow wiped the powder off. Remembering that minor fletch contact is inevitable, you can make adjustments from here to alleviate the problem.

7. Conduct close-range paper testing.

PAPER TESTING

Paper testing, or paper tuning, is the best method around for gauging arrow flight. Using the paper-tuning method, you can tune arrow flight with either field points or broadheads. When setting up a new hunting bow, I tune it first with field points, then go out and shoot a bit, getting used to the bow and setting my sight pins for the distances I like—20, 30, 40, and 50 yards. Then, a bit before hunting season, I retune the bow, this time with broadheads, then go out and reset my sight pins. You'll probably have to make a few minor tuning adjustments when switching from field points to broadheads. They should be just that—minor adjustments. Sometimes you don't need to make changes at all.

Shooting your bow through a chrono-graph at your local archery pro shop during the tuning process will let you know exactly how fast your arrows are flying. This informa-tion can be invaluable when visualizing arrow trajectory in the field.

To paper-tune the bow, you'll need a frame to hold the paper and paper to shoot through. There are commercial frames available, but you can make your own out of plywood or do what I do when I'm in the field—use an old cardboard box with the bottom and top cut out. The box should be at least 18 x 18 inches, although I like a box that's 24 x 24 inches. I tape my paper over the holes—old newspaper works okay, but I prefer white butcher paper—then set the box on a stump, small dirt mound, pair of saw horses, or some other support that will prop it up solidly at chest height. Three feet behind the paper rack, place a target butt to stop your arrows.

The illustration on page 72, provided by arrow maker Easton Technical Products, helps explain the paper-tuning process. The goal is to achieve a perfect bullet-hole tear through the paper. Keep two things in mind here. One, you will find small imperfect tears on some shots, even when the bow is perfectly tuned, due to hand torque on the riser. When you are paper-tuning, take your time and use as close to perfect shooting form as you can. Two, not all bowhunters find that they get the best accuracy with the perfect bullet-hole tear. Many like to have an arrow that tears slightly high and to the left of center (for right-handed shooters.) The final judge on your bow setup is how well it groups broadhead-tipped arrows at the end of your own maximum personal shooting range.

Paper Tuning Arrow Test

The Paper Tuning Arrow Test is a good basic bow tuning method for all three types of shooting styles—Recurve with finger release (RF), Compound with finger release (CF) and Compound with release aid (CR).

- Firmly attach a sheet of paper to a frame type rack approximately 24" x 24" (60 x 60 cm).
- Position the center of the paper about shoulder height with a target mat about six feet (1.5m) behind the paper to stop the arrows.
- Stand approximately six feet (1.8m) from the paper.
- Shoot a fletched arrow through the center of the paper with the arrow at shoulder height.
- Observe how the paper is torn.

A. Tear A indicates good arrow flight. The point and fletching enter the same hole.

NOTE: Try the following instructions in order, one at a time.

B. Tear B indicates a low nocking point. To correct, raise the nocking point 1/16" (1.6mm) at a time and repeat the procedure until the low vertical tear is eliminated.

C. Tear C indicates a high nocking point. Clearance problem or (for release aid) a mismatched arrow spine. To correct, lower the nocking point 1/16" (1.6mm) at a time until the high tear is eliminated. If the problem remains unchanged, the disturbance is probably caused by a lack of Clearance or (for release aid) a mismatched arrow spine. CR only—if no Clearance problem exists try:

1. A more flexible arrow rest blade or reducing downward spring tension on launcher rests.
2. Decreasing or increasing peak bow weight.
3. Reducing the amount the shaft overhangs the contact point on the arrow rest.
4. Using a stiffer arrow shaft.

NOTE: The following instructions are for right-handed archers. Reverse for left-handed archers.

The best way to tune your bow is to shoot arrows through blank white paper. Attach a sheet of paper to a sturdy frame (24 × 24 inches is ideal). Position the center of the paper about shoulder height with a target mat about six feet behind the paper, to stop your arrows. Stand six feet from the paper, and shoot a fletched arrow through the center of the paper. **Tear A** indicates ideal arrow flight, with the point and fletching entering the same hole. **Tear B** indicates a low nocking point, with the point entering the paper above the fletching. To correct, slightly raise your nocking point until the tear resembles tear A. **Tear C** indicates a high nocking point. To correct, lower the nocking point until you achieve tear A. If lowering the point does not work, you may have a clearance problem. *Illustration by Christopher Seubert.*

Some people claim they can tune their bows so that both their field points and broadheads hit exactly the same place. Don't believe it. I've tuned a lot of bows over the years, and the number I've had that could do that you can count on one hand and have some fingers left over. It's not important that they do, though. What is important is that you achieve dartlike arrow flight with broadheads, then set your sight pins so they correspond exactly to how your shafts are flying with the broadheads attached. After all, you won't be shooting at game with field tips. Who cares where they hit when the season's on?

Prior to hunting season, begin shooting your broadhead-tipped shafts at targets, both to set your sight pins and to make sure that each broadhead-tipped arrow in your quiver flies straight and true.

First, I make sure both my arrow nocks and broadheads are perfectly aligned with the shaft. To check the broadheads, give the shaft the "spin test." Simply hold the shaft vertically and place the tip of the broadhead on a hard, flat surface. Now lightly hold the shaft near the fletching and spin it on this point like a top. Watch the area where the shaft's insert and the broadhead meet. If it appears to wobble, there's an alignment problem and you can be sure this shaft will not fly as accurately as possible. This wobble can be caused by a couple of things, including a broadhead ferrule that did not come perfectly straight from the factory, loose blades, a shaft insert that is not perfectly aligned inside the shaft itself, or a slightly bent arrow. To correct this I change to a different broadhead and try the test again, and am not satisfied until there in no discernible wobble. If I find a bad ferrule or shaft, I discard it.

Next, conduct an accuracy test. Some people alternate shooting one shaft with a field point, then one with a broadhead, at different targets, until three shafts of each kind have been shot. They then compare the group size of both three-shot cluster (group size is measured between the inside points where the two shafts furthest apart struck the target). Your broadhead groups should be close to the same size as the field point group—no more than a couple of inches larger. You should shoot your test groups, at least five times, and shoot them at your maximum effective shooting range.

If you don't want to go through all that, just shoot your broadheads. If your groups are nice and tight, you're getting good broadhead flight. One thing to watch for is the same arrow always grouping farthest away from your group's center. If it is, you may have a problem with that particular arrow. If you find a "bad arrow" try a different broadhead and see how it groups. If the arrow continues to be a poor shooter, discard it.

Once I find half a dozen arrow shafts and broadheads that group well, I mark them with an indelible felt-tip pen, giving both the shaft and the broadhead the same number. That way if I ever take the broadheads off the shafts for transportation, cleaning, or replacing the broadhead blades with new ones before hunting, I can match them up again. During my practice sessions it seems I always find one or two shaft/broadhead combinations that really fly like laser beams. These I designate my No. 1 and No. 2 arrows, and I make sure they are placed in my quiver in such a way that I will automatically use them first in the field.

Paper-tuning your bow is not black magic. It can be time-consuming and sometimes frustrating. However, the best advice anyone can give you about putting together a new bow-and-arrow setup is this: Don't head afield without tuning your bow to give you precise, laser-beam arrow flight. This will breed accuracy, which helps give you confidence in your ability to make the shot when the chips are down. And that's what it's all about.

HOW TO SHOOT YOUR BOW

8

You don't have to be a star athlete to shoot a bow accurately. In fact, I know quite a few successful bowhunters who have trouble tying their laces in the morning, are always tripping over things in the woods, and are so mechanically impaired they find changing batteries in their flashlights a real chore. If the truth be known, I'm one of them. These folks will probably never win a major target shoot, but they are excellent field shots who, when the chips are down, consistently place their broadhead-tipped arrows into the boiler room of whatever animal they're hunting.

Their formula for success is really pretty simple. They all shoot matched tackle that has been precisely tuned, and they have their sight pins set the way they want them. They learned the basics of bow shooting from someone who knew how to teach them. And they spent countless hours practicing before the season, fine-tuning their muscles and skills.

Although accurate bow shooting is not that tough, there is a risk of learning to shoot a bow incorrectly. Unless you begin slowly with proper instruction, you can develop poor habits and lousy shooting form that could plague you all your life. That's why I recommend that beginning bowhunters spend some time at their local archery pro shop, where the resident pro can teach you the correct way to shoot from the get-go. Bad habits are difficult to break. It's always better to learn from someone who knows how to do it right and has experience helping beginners get started.

If there is one key word in accurately shooting a bow, it is this—*relax*. Don't be taut and tense. Instead, relax both your muscles and your mind as you shoot. The best bow shots keep their muscles working naturally for them, not tensely against them. They also relax their minds, forgetting about stress and strain. There's no pressure on you to outshoot the next guy here. You're simply trying to do the best you can do. A relaxed shooting form breeds consistency, the key to accurate shooting.

Before going into how to hold the bow and release the string, here are some questions you may want answered.

HOW SOON SHOULD I BEGIN PRACTICING?

The best bow shots I know shoot at least a few arrows every day, all year round. Shooting a bow is an athletic skill, and the way to be the best bow shooter you can be is to keep your form sharp and muscles tuned. However, for a variety of reasons, most of us can't shoot on a daily basis throughout the year. If that's the case with you, you should begin shooting at least a little bit three or four months prior to hunting season. This will give you plenty of time to iron out kinks in your form as well as find and fix problems with your tackle. It is unethical to simply grab your bow out of the closet, shoot a few practice arrows a week or two before opening day, then head afield. We all owe it to both the game we hunt and our fellow bowhunters to take time enough to prepare our shooting skills so that when the time comes, we can make an accurate shot and clean, humane kill.

TOO MUCH OF A GOOD THING?

You're determined to master this bow-shooting thing, and so you think the best way to do this is to shoot a bazillion practice arrows, right? Not necessarily. In fact, it is easy to practice *too much* with your bow and arrow. Overpractice is one of the best ways I know of to develop sloppy shooting habits. That's because your arm, back, and shoulder muscles will become sore and fatigued with too much shooting. When that happens you'll see your groups open up and shooting form falter, which leads to a lack of confidence.

When you feel tired, take a break. Most beginners have trouble shooting more than 20 to 40 arrows before fading. When I have been shooting for a few months, I find I can shoot perhaps 80 to 100 arrows in a day's time before I wear down. Also, it is a good idea not to shoot a lot of arrows day in and day out. Taking a day off helps your muscles to recover and, just as important, your mind to recover, too. When I begin my own serious preseason practice sessions four months before opening day, I shoot only a dozen arrows for the first few times out. As time goes by the number of arrows I shoot during practice sessions increases. I also try never to shoot a lot of arrows two days in a row. If I shoot 50 to 80 shafts one day, the next day I might only shoot 10 to 15—if I shoot at all.

When you are practicing, take your time between shots. Shooting a bow is not a game of speed, like basketball. Instead, like golf, it's as much a game of calculation and mental preparation as it is physically making the shot. I like to shoot an arrow, then take a few minutes before the next shot. This gives me time to relax my muscles and go through my mental checklist of proper shooting form. When you shoot too quickly, it is easy to get into a groove for making the same shooting form mistakes over and over until they become ingrained habits and thus difficult to break.

One final note on bow-shooting practice. Highly trained athletes have their good days and their bad days, and so will you when it comes to shooting your bow. Some days it seems that your arrows are magically drawn to the center of the target. On others, it's tough to find your posterior with both hands. Don't worry about it. When I'm having "one of those days," I quit shooting and go do something else. There's no use fighting it, so why try? It's better to retreat and come back a day or two later, mind refreshed, and muscles relaxed.

HOW FAR AWAY SHOULD I PRACTICE?

There's a tendency for beginning bowhunters to want to fling arrows from long distance. Heck, it's fun. But the best way to improve your shooting skills is to begin practice sessions at relatively short range. Somewhere between 10 and 15 yards is good. After your shooting form improves, move out to 20 yards. When teaching beginners how to release an arrow, instructors often have their students stand in front of a target only 10 *feet* away and shoot with their eyes closed so that they can mentally visualize their form and not worry about where the arrow is hitting.

As you become more skilled in your shooting, move farther away from the target. Soon you'll be able to consistently make good shots at 40 yards or more. We'll talk more about establishing your own maximum effective shooting range in Chapter 9. For now, suffice it to say that practicing at longer distances is the best way to force yourself to concentrate on every facet of accurately shooting your bow. Once you begin making shots at 40 yards, you'll be surprised how easy those 20 yarders become. I'm a firm believer that bowhunters should practice shooting well past the distances at which they anticipate taking shots at game. Not that they should ever shoot at an animal past their own "comfort zone." It's just that once basic shooting form and skills have been mastered, long-distance practice is the best way to improve your overall ability to make the shot at any distance.

BOW SHOOTING BY THE NUMBERS

In the military they tell you to do certain things "by the numbers." That means there's a right way (*their* way!) and a wrong way to accomplish the task. Shooting a bow is the same. The basic steps are stance, draw, anchor, aim, release, and follow-through.

STANCE

Most top bow shots prefer a sort of open stance, with their back foot set at about 90 degrees to the target and the front foot set at about 60 degrees. Spread your feet 12 to 18 inches apart, and get comfortable. Your torso should be straight up and down—don't lean forward or backward. As you lift the bow, you should not have to cock your head to see the sights. The key is to have

Proper shooting form is the basis for all successful bowhunting. The best place to learn is at your local archery pro shop, where expert instruction is available along with help in setting up and maintaining your equipment.

your bow set up so that it will fit your stance, not the other way around.

Proper hand position on the bow handle cannot be overemphasized. When placing your hand on the bow, do so in a consistent manner shot after shot. Variations in hand placement and pressure can cause inconsistencies in arrow flight, which will hurt accuracy. Keep a natural, relaxed wrist. The major pressure should occur in the webbing between the thumb and forefinger. Lightly grip the bow with your index and middle fingers, taking care not to choke the handle. Avoid pressuring the handle with your palm, as this will create torque, which will definitely alter arrow flight.

If you shoot with your fingers, the most common method of string hand placement is to use the first three fingers, placing the index finger over the arrow nock and the other two under the nock. If you use a release aid, the position of your hand will be dictated by the style of release you're using.

DRAWING THE BOW

To draw the bow, simply raise your bow arm into shooting position and smoothly draw the bowstring back to your anchor spot. Remember that you shouldn't have to "cheat"—that is, lift the bow above the vertical to get it drawn back. If you have to cheat, you need to reduce the draw weight until you can properly draw the string back. Over time, as your bow-pulling muscles strengthen, you'll be able to pull more draw weight than in the beginning.

It is important to keep your bow arm relaxed during the draw. Once you get the bow up and drawn back, the bow arm should lock into place in a relaxed fashion. The shoulder should be pulled down, forcing the humerus into the shoulder socket. You should also rotate your forearm so that the wrist is in the vertical position, which is the best position for maximum bowstring clearance. Experiment with different bow hand, bow arm, and foot positions as you take your stance and draw the bow until you find the combination that's most comfortable.

ANCHOR

A consistent shot-to-shot anchor point is critical to consistent accuracy. There are several ways to anchor the bowstring. When shooting with fingers, I like to place the tip of my index finger in the corner of my mouth. Some people place the thumb knuckle under the chin. Anchor points with mechanical release aids vary by style of release. When shooting a wrist-strap caliper-type release—the most popular in use today—most shooters place the big knuckle of the thumb solidly under the rear of the jawbone. It really doesn't matter where you anchor the bowstring, only that you do it the same way every time.

If you use a peep sight, as most present-day compound shooters do, bring the bowstring back until it touches the tip of your nose when you draw and anchor. Having the peep properly placed between the strands of the bowstring will do two things. First, it allows you to clearly see your sight pins through the peep without cocking your head to one side or the other. Second, it acts as a secondary anchor point, which helps reinforce your primary anchor point.

AIMING

Aiming the arrow is not rocket science. You simply select the right sight pin for the distance, place it in the center of the peep sight, put it on the center of the target, hold it steady for a moment, and release.

The keys to aiming are consistency and smoothness. Smart bowhunters place their pin on the target the same way every time. Some like to line up their spot, then move the sight pin up from the bottom of the target to the right location before releasing. Others like to come from the top down. Both work well, but you'll find your shooting is better if you do it the same way every time. Also important is to smoothly move the pin on target instead of in a herky-jerky motion. Shooting a bow should be fluid, not break dancing.

You'll also find that it is impossible to hold the sight pin completely steady on the target. It's going to bounce and jump around some. Don't fight this. Professional tournament champion and top-notch bowhunter Randy Ulmer advises shooters to let the sight pin "float" over and around the target, releasing the arrow when it floats over the right spot. "Through patience, you'll just know when the exact moment to release the arrow comes," Ulmer said. "If you fight it, you'll get so tense trying to do something that is really impossible that you'll never be as accurate a shot as you can be."

You'll also find that you cannot focus your eye on both the target and the sight pin at the same time. You'll shoot best if you focus on the sight pin, not the animal. This is what top-notch competitive pistol shooters do. As I settle my sight pin, I focus on the target first, picking the spot on the animal I want to hit. I then let my subconscious remember that spot and focus on the sight pin as I place it precisely where I want my arrow to go.

On the target range, you'll be able to shoot from marked distances that correspond to the common sight pin settings of 20, 30, 40, and 50 yards. In the field, however, you'll often find that, often as not, you'll be shooting at an animal that is an odd distance away. Instead of 20 or 30 yards away, it's actually 25 yards, for example. If you use a common pin-type bow sight, you'll then have to do what I call "shooting between the pins."

On shots such as these, I simply split the difference between my pins when aiming. That is, instead of pulling the 20-yard pin on the spot I want to hit, I raise it slightly above the spot, keeping the 30-yard pin just below it. This places the space between the pins vertically dead-on the target. Also, by drawing an imaginary line between the two pins I can line up the shot horizontally. This may sound weird at first, but it works. Be sure to practice this aiming skill during your practice sessions so you'll know how to do it when the time comes.

THE RELEASE

A smooth, consistent bowstring release is paramount to accurate shooting. If you shoot with your fingers, simply relax the fingers and let the string slip smoothly away. Do no throw the string hand open or pluck the string like a guitar, two common mistakes.

Because releasing the string consistently shot after shot with fingers is so difficult, mechanical release aids have become the method of string release for more than 80 percent of today's bowhunters. With the simple squeeze of a trigger or press of a button, the machine that is the release sends the string off with the same amount of pressure shot after shot. That this translates into more accurate shooting is evident in the world of serious target shooting, where release shooters were given their own classification after they began beating fingers shooters virtually every time out.

Release shooting isn't a no-brainer, though. It is easy to punch or jerk the trigger or button, which defeats the purpose of the exercise. Approach the triggering mechanism the same way every time. To prevent accidentally setting off the trigger of my release prematurely, I keep my finger behind the trigger when drawing the bow, and don't place it on the front of the trigger it-self until my sight pin is settling onto my spot.

FOLLOW-THROUGH

In all athletic endeavors—swinging a golf club, shooting a basket-ball, throwing a football—follow-through makes sure you won't drop your bow or force it to the side before the arrow has cleared, which will send the shaft off-target.

To follow through, concentrate on continuing to aim at the target after the string has been released. Sounds simple, doesn't it? Yet following through is one of the most difficult pieces of the accuracy equation for most archers. In the excitement of shooting at a big-game animal, the tendency for most people—myself included—is to drop that bow out of the way so we can watch the arrow strike the target. That is a sure-fine formula for missing. Instead, concentrate on keeping your bow arm straight, looking for the spin of the fletching through your peep sight. It is this conscious follow-through that will ensure that all your practice and preparation up to this point will not have been in vain.

PRACTICE IN THE FIELD

There's more to successful game shooting than practicing at bull's-eye targets set at known distances. You'll need some realistic field practice, too. I begin by shooting on the target range from a position other than standing straight up. These include kneeling, sitting on a stool, and twisting my torso into odd angles from all three positions. This helps me simulate realistic shooting positions encountered when hunting from the ground. To prepare myself for tree-stand hunting, I climb onto the deck of my house and shoot down at targets. I also set a tree stand at the same height as the stands I'll hunt out of in the fall, with targets scattered near the stand at various distances.

"Stump shooting" is another terrific way to practice field shooting. Here you simply walk around the woods, shooting blunt-tipped arrows at rotten tree stumps, tufts of grass, mud banks—whatever you can safely shoot at without destroying the arrow. By pretending these targets are actually big bucks or bulls, you can not only hone field shooting skills, you can learn how to accurately estimate range. This technique also teaches you your limitations.

Finally, don't overlook shooting at 3-D targets. These are realistic targets built to the same size and shape as a variety of game animals. Some bowhunters purchase their own 3-D targets (they're pricey!), but many archery clubs have 3-D target ranges already set up. Here they hold both informal practice days and tournaments, which are great fun and excellent practice. Your local archery pro shop should be able to direct you to any 3-D courses in your area.

BOWHUNTING GEAR

9

In his classic work *A Sand Country Almanac,* Aldo Leopold called the new generation of hunters "gadgeteers' for their love of new technology and propensity for using it in place of old-fashioned woodsmanship. This was back in the 1940s! What would Leopold think of today's sportsmen and their mind-boggling array of high-tech equipment?

No doubt about it, today's hunters like their "stuff." Smart and experienced bowhunters, however, have learned to take it all with a grain of salt. They eyeball each new gizmo with a careful eye. As Euripides said back in 412 B.C., "Man's most valuable trait is a judicious sense of what not to believe." You, too, should be skeptical of gadget manufacturers who claim their products can do amazing things.

That said, several product categories do offer modern bowhunters superior performance and the reliability of the sunrise. Here's a look at some of those you'll want to consider.

CAMOUFLAGE

Despite all the hype, camouflage will not make you the invisible man. Yet judicious use of camouflage will definitely help your bowhunting scorecard. But with all the different patterns out there, how do you decide which is best?

Although there is still much debate how much color big-game animals can see—if any—most authorities agree that deer, elk, and bears see the world in black, white, and shades of gray. For that reason, I believe the two things that give us away to big game animals the most are scent and movement. I once told Bill Jordan, who invented the various Realtree and Advantage camo patterns, that I had the perfect pattern that would put him out of business. "Tell me," he said, "and we'll make it." My idea? Take the old red and black checkered wool shirt your granddad wore in the woods. In the red squares, put black writing; in the black squares, put red writing. One should say, "Watch the Wind," the other, "Don't Move." Bill said something like, "Don't *ever* tell anyone that!"

That said, it is important that bowhunters cover the shiny parts of their exposed skin, including hands, ears, and face with gloves, a face mask, or a camouflage cream such as CarboMask. I prefer camouflage with a more open pattern as opposed to one with a tight pattern. At a distance, the tight patterns tend to look like a solid dark blob, while the open patterns help break up your outline. I also try to match the prevailing foliage color whenever possible.

I always wear camo when bowhunting, and I believe that together with playing the wind and not moving at the wrong time, it will help me stay hidden. The additional confidence alone is worth the price of admission.

OPTICS

All bowhunters need a quality binocular. There are many makes and models of binoculars out there, and serious hunters should purchase the best optics they can afford. Higher-priced optics have higher quality glass that translates into a clearer picture, especially when light conditions are poor.

Binocular prices vary widely. For example, the very best 10 x 40 binos from such companies as Bausch & Lomb, Zeiss, Leica, Swarovski, Leupold, and Steiner will run between $750 and $1,000. Similar binos from Simmons, Nikon, Tasco, and Bushnell cost somewhere between $150 and $200. You can find them for half that price, too. When considering price, remember that you're making a purchase that will last you a lifetime. Factored over many years, the initial price of a top-end binocular isn't really all that much.

Smallish compact binoculars are not recommended. That's because they are too small to use enough available light in low-light conditions—when game animals are most active—to make them very useful. Standard-sized binoculars in powers such as 7 x 35, 8 x 30, 8 x 40, 10 x 40, and 10 x 50 are the most useful all-around sizes. If you hunt in the West, where judging game at long range is important, you'll need a tripod-mounted spotting scope. Scopes with a variable eyepiece in 15-45X and 20-60X are my favorite.

TRAIL TIMERS

One of the most useful items I've played with in recent years is a trail timer. These gizmos use a beam of light that, when broken by an animal passing through the beam, records the date and time of passage. Inexpensive models cost less than $25, but record only one passing. Models costing between $100 and $300 can record several hundred passings before you have to reset them. The Cam-Trakker and Trail-Master even take the animal's picture.

Trail timers can help you determine when animals are passing along certain trails or when black bears are hitting bait stations. They also let you know how much activity is occurring on a given trail at a given time. Such data can be useful in deciding where and when to set up. I use them even in the off-season as I try to piece together the patterns deer and other animals are using on a specific piece of property.

DAY PACKS

You're going to need some sort of pack to carry your stuff. Obviously you'll need a different size and design of pack for backpacking trips as opposed to day trips to a tree stand.

For most day hunts, either a fanny or day pack will suffice. Fanny packs are worn across the lower back and secured with a web belt. Day packs are worn over the shoulders, like the ones your kids tote their school books in. Whichever you choose, make sure your pack has enough room for your basic accessories, some drinks and snacks for all-day sits, and extra clothes. I also carry a screw-in step in my pack, which allows me to hang it next to my tree stand. This makes it accessible with minimum movement and keeps it out from under my feet.

Choose a fanny pack made from quiet fabrics such as fleece or Stealth Cloth. Zippered closures are quieter to open and close than Velcro.

Wide belts and shoulder straps help spread the load, and exterior web straps that allow you to strap on a heavy jacket while hiking are a great feature. There are several excellent hunting pack makers, including Badlands, Crooked Horn Outfitters, White Buffalo Outdoors, and Fieldline.

TREE STANDS

The tree stand is the bowhunter's best friend. We'll talk more about using them in Chapter 10. Basically, there are six types of tree stands: portable, climbing, ladder, tree sling, tripod, and homemade.

Portable or fixed-position stands are the most popular type. They feature a platform and seat attached by a metal pole, all of which is attached to the tree trunk on top with either chain or nylon webbing, and supported on the bottom by either screw-in T-screws or built-in spikes. Tree steps or ladders are required to climb the tree when using them. There are more different makes, models, sizes, and styles of fixed-position stands than there are of any other. Fixed-position stands are also the most versatile, because they can be used safely in virtually any type, size, and height tree. Many bowhunters like smaller fixed-position stands because they present a smaller outline against the tree trunk than larger stands. To use them you'll also need some tree steps or a portable ladder system.

Climbing stands are popular in areas where there are lots of tall, straight trees with few limbs, such as oaks, birch and the like. They are designed for quick, quiet climbing without the use of tree steps or ladders. They generally have two pieces, with the hunter raising and securing the top piece with his arms, then lifting and securing the bottom piece with his feet. They are usually heavier and bulkier than fixed-position stands.

Climbers are excellent when the hunter is scouting on the move, prepared to set up and hunt hot sign that day. They are quick to set up, allowing the hunter to find his tree, assemble the stand, and climb into position in a matter of a few minutes. This also makes small adjustments in stand location during the hunting day both easy and practical. The downside is that they are impractical to use in trees with lots of large limbs or crooked trunks. You also must remember to connect the bottom section to the top section with a safety rope or cord. If the bottom portion slips off your feet and falls to the ground without the safety cord, you'll be left hanging—literally.

Ladder stands are basically metal ladders secured to the tree, with a small seat/foot rest built into the top of the ladder. Ladder stands are easy to climb and are most popular on private land, where their bulk and weight are not a factor with hunters who leave them set up all season. Ladders are growing in popularity each year because they are easy to set up and generally very safe. When you begin securing the ladder to the tree, you must take care that it will not roll off the trunk at the top, a potential problem on small-diameter trees with slick trunks. Ladders also generally only permit you to get no more than 12 to 14 feet off the ground, with many only rising 10 feet up. They also create a large silhouette against the tree trunk.

Tree slings permit the hunter to sit in a sling held in place by several nylon web straps and/or rope. Slings allow the hunter to remain close to the tree trunk, reducing his outline, and also quietly maneuver around the tree trunk and change his shot angle, depending on the direction from which game is approaching. These are graduate-level stands that take some getting used to. They are popular with bowhunters because of their versatility and the small outline generated against the tree trunk. Most hunters use a pair of screw-in tree steps as foot rests once the sling has been set up, which makes waiting more comfortable.

Tripod stands are most popular in Texas and portions of the Southwest, where the tall trees needed to use more conventional tree stands are few and far between. Tripods are just that—three legs joined at the top, on which a rotating seat or shooting house is placed. These are monstrous stands and stick out like a sore thumb unless they are set up inside or adjacent to a small tree like a cedar. If they are set up and left for a long period of time, though, game generally will get used to their presence. Hunters sitting in an open-area tripod with a seat on top must take great care not to fidget because they have little or no cover around them. Tripod stands are stable, safe stands, and easy to get in and out of. They work well when set overlooking large green fields, feeders (where legal), and open-country water holes.

Homemade stands are those constructed by hunters of wood, nails, and whatever else they may have lying around. Extreme caution should be used before climbing into a homemade stand you're not familiar with. Rotting wood and loose steps have been the cause of more than one serious accident.

One final note about tree stands and their use: Never, ever use a tree stand without wearing an approved safety belt or harness. Every year several people are killed, and hundreds more seriously injured, in tree-stand accidents. Most were not wearing a safety belt or harness at the time. You don't want to be one of them.

ANCILLARY GEAR

There are several small items you'll need for basic tree-stand deer hunting. Other hunting trips for other game will, of course, require refinements in this list, which includes:

Small hunting knife: For field-dressing your deer.

Pruning shears: For snipping off small branches.

Compact saw: For trimming large branches. Browning, Uncle Mike's and Game Tracker make good ones.

Pull rope: For hauling your weapon and day pack up and down the tree. Nylon parachute cord works well.

Bow holder: Either hooks that screw into the tree trunk or holders that clamp onto the stand's platform keep your bow handy and your hands free.

Headlamp: Better than a flashlight, it keeps your hands free for climbing up and down the tree in the dark.

Flagging: Can be used to flag the trail into the stand so it is easy to find in the dark, or as an aid when tracking bow-shot game. Fluorescent stick-on dots that glow in the light of a flash-light also work for this.

Wind detector: A talc-filled puff bottle or butane lighter works, but tying a piece of thread with small downy feather on a tree branch will allow you to monitor subtle wind changes constantly. Knight & Hale's Wind Floater, a small pouch filled with downy-light fluff pieces, is an excellent wind detector.

Walkie-talkie: Compact radios are great for communicating with your buddies, calling for help to drag out your deer, and in case of emergencies. Motorola is the leader in sportsman's radios for this type.

Butane lighter: For wind checking, but also as a survival item.

Hunting license/tags: Required to be on your person by law. I carry mine in a plastic baggie for protection against the elements.

Pee bottle: 'nuff said.

BASIC BOWHUNTING TECHNIQUES 10

Volumes have been written about bowhunting various big-game species. We don't have the space to delve into the nuances of successfully bowhunting everything from deer to elk to bears, but we can lay down the groundwork for bowhunting just about any big-game animal in North America. How? Simply put, there are some basic truisms in all bowhunting. These apply regardless of what you're hunting or where you're hunting it.

First, remember the goal of all bowhunters: to put themselves into a position to take a close-range shot at an undisturbed animal. To that end, you must spot the animal before it sees, hears, or smells you. Once you find it, you must not only get close enough for the shot, but also be able to draw your bow and release your arrow undetected.

There are four basic bowhunting methods: hunting from a stand, spot and stalk hunting, still hunting, and calling. Before you actually go hunting, though, it's best to understand a little bit about how to penetrate an animal's sensory defenses.

DEFEAT THE SENSES

Most big-game animals, but especially ungulates such as deer and elk, live in a world of smell. They depend on their sense of smell as the first line of defense against predators, which includes bowhunters. Most experienced bowhunters will tell you that if your quarry spots you or hears you, you might get away with it. But if they smell you, the party's over. They will turn and run as fast as their little legs can carry them.

To help defeat an animal's sense of smell, many bowhunters use cover or masking scents. I have never found these to be all that effective, though. Smart bowhunters will, however, take great pains to eliminate as much foul-smelling human odor as possible. They do this by bathing with non-scent soap, washing their clothes in the same, and storing their clothing in a plastic bag so it won't pick up odors at home or in the truck. They may go an extra mile and wear scent-blocking clothing and rubber-bottom boots. Both of which have worked well for me at times. Above all else, they are meticulous wind-dopers. That is, they are constantly monitoring the wind direction. They know that the most important thing they can do to be successful is to keep the wind in their face so that it does not blow their smell to the animal's radar-like nose. Rule number one in all big-game bowhunting is simply this: Keep the wind right at all times.

Many bowhunters employ scent-eliminating sprays to kill the bacteria that cause human odors, but the best defense against being smelled by game is to remain upwind.

Using a small puff bottle filled with unscented talc is a good way to monitor wind direction.

Smart bowhunters also don't ever make human-like noises in the woods. That includes talking; coughing; banging metal on metal; wearing scratchy, noisy clothing like denim and nylon; slamming car doors near stand sites; and so on. They do their best to slip through the woods on cat's feet, knowing that the hearing of most game animals is so much more acute than a human's that we really can't comprehend it. If the game hears you coming, it will simply slip away. You'll never even know it was there.

Finally, successful bowhunters don't let their quarry see them. That means blending into their surroundings with the judicious use of camouflage, eliminating shiny objects from their gear, and meticulously camouflaging their stand sites. It also means moving slowly, carefully scanning ahead for an animal before taking the next step. Watch a cat stalk a bird in your backyard and see how slowly it moves. Cats would make excellent bowhunters.

TAKE A STAND

Taking a stand is the most effective bowhunting method ever devised. That's because you're letting the animal come to you, not going to it. This, in turn, means that you don't have to move at all as the game approaches, both helping you stay hidden and giving you a chance to size the animal up and get ready to make the shot. The effectiveness of stand hunting is evident when you realize that more than 90 percent of all whitetail bowhunters hunt from some sort of stand, and more than 80 percent of all Pope & Young record book whitetails have been taken by archers hunting from stands.

Stands are also conducive to short-range shots. If you set a stand in a relatively thick area on a known travel route, deer and other game will pass by your stand well within your comfortable shooting range. Most stands are set to give the archer shots of between 15 and 25 yards. Another advantage of stand hunting is that even if the animal walks past your stand and you either don't get a shot or choose not to take one, the animal can proceed undisturbed. That means it will never know someone was in its living room and hence will have no reason to change its habits. You can then confidently hunt the same stand again and again.

There are two basic stand types—tree stands and ground blinds. Ground blinds are simply that—blinds built on the ground in places where game is likely to appear. Tree stands are more common—and more effective. There are two reasons for this. One, they elevate you off the ground which is a tremendous help in keeping animals from smelling you. Second, by elevating yourself above the animal's line of sight, it is easier to draw and shoot your bow without being seen. One final word on stands: For your stand to be effective, you must be comfortable. You have to spend countless hours sitting in your stand. Unless you do this without doing the hully-gully, you'll never get a shot. The game will see you moving, and it will be all over before it ever begins.

The downside of stand hunting is the same thing that makes it so effective: it's static. If you place your stand in the wrong place, you are going to be bored silly. That means you have to scout the hunting area to locate places where game is likely to pass during legal shooting hours.

I key in on two basic types of places to set tree stands: food sources such as mast crops—which for most whitetail hunters mean acorns—as well as food plots, green fields, honeysuckle, persimmons, standing corn, alfalfa fields, and so on are dynamite stand sites. In any given area, deer have what we call "preferred food sources," which refers to a specific food source that, when available, the deer flock to like kids to candy. Find out what this is in your hunting area, then scout until you find where it's available, and you'll have a great place to set a stand.

Funnels are areas along an animal's travel route where the nature of the cover is such that it pinches, or constricts, the likely places the animal will pass through on its daily journey. Likely funnel locations include along fences, fence crossings, saddles, creek bottoms, and edges where thick cover meets thinner cover. I like to hunt funnels located between thick bedding cover and a preferred food source.

Rutting areas are also good places to set stands. Whitetail scrapes and rub lines can be excellent rut-hunting stand sites. Wallows are good places to set a tree stand for elk. But remember this: During the rut, males go to the females, and females daily go to food. That's why food sources are such dynamite stand sites all season.

In dry, arid country, water holes can be superb stand sites. Water hole hunting is more important to western bowhunters pursuing pronghorns, elk, mule deer, and Coues deer than it is to eastern whitetail hunters.

Regardless of where you set your stand, there are a few basic tenets you must follow. First, set your stand so that you can approach and leave it with little chance of game seeing, hearing, or smelling you. Second, you have to be able to get a clear shot from your stand. That often means pruning bush and/or tree limbs to clear shooting lanes. Only remove necessary branches, however. You want to clear some lanes, but not alter the look of the woods so much that game can recognize the changes, or cut down so many limbs that you remove all your own cover. (Trust me, deer *do* look up. You need some cover up there!) Set your stand on the downward side of the trail you think the game will approach from. Even though you're off the ground, chances are good they'll smell you if they come in from upwind. Many bowhunters set more than one stand in a good spot, choosing the specific one they'll hunt on a given day according to that day's wind direction.

SPOT AND STALK HUNTING

Spot and stalk hunting is best used in open country like that found in the West, where the nature of the terrain and lower animal densities can make it a better choice than stand hunting. However, spot and stalk hunting can be effective in semi-open country, too. I've taken several animals—elk, blacktail deer, mule deer, and wild hogs—in country where visibility was much less than a quarter mile.

In this game, you find a spot that gives a good overall view of the country and use your optics to locate game to stalk. It can take hours and hours of meticulous glassing, but once you find the animal you want, it's time to plan the stalk.

And plan you must. Too many bowhunters simply dive off the hill with no real plan and ultimately blow their chance. It's best to first try to anticipate where the animal is heading. Use your binoculars to try to dope the wind by watching blowing grasses or hanging moss. If you see deer or elk moving and can get ahead of their path with the wind right, you might be able to intercept them by hiding behind some natural cover.

If I can't pick them off this way, I like to wait until the animal has bedded for the day, then put on a stalk. Step one is to plan a good stalking routine, again using your optics to guide you. Identify easily recognizable landmarks both along this route and near where the animal has bedded. This is critical, because things never look the same once you get to them as they did through your glasses. Also, look for other animals. Many a stalk has been blown by stumbling over an animal you never saw.

Remember thermal currents, which are critical in stalking bedded game. Generally speaking, thermals take the wind down the slope in the early morning and late afternoon and evening, and carry the wind up the slope from mid-morning and late afternoon. When stalking, use the thermals to help keep your scent from the game.

The key to a successful stalk is to not move too fast. You might hike fast or even run to initially get into position, but the final stalk should be made at a snail's pace. Deliberately set your feet and hands down one at a time. Move any dry sticks or potential rolling rocks out of the way before taking the next step. When you get the urge to rush in and get it over with, remember the question Larry Jones, a call maker, video producer, and one heck of a bowhunter, asks himself when the urge to hurry overtakes him: "Why am I in such a hurry to blow this stalk?"

As you get close to the animal, relocating it can take some time. Use your binoculars to pick apart the terrain and look for a piece of the animal, like an antler tine, shiny nose, twitching ear, or white rump patch. Once I've found him, I slowly creep in to my own maximum personal shooting range, and go no farther. That's where I want to shoot from. Trying to get any closer only ups the odds that something will go wrong. If I have a clear shot at the bedded animal's vitals, I'll shoot. I'll wait for him to stand up, which will give me a better chance to hit both lungs.

STILL HUNTING

Still hunting is one tough way to bowhunt. Unlike spot and stalk hunting, in which you first spot the animal before meticulously planning how you're going to stalk it, in still hunting you simply slowly sneak along, making no noise, and hope to spot an animal before he spots you.

Successful still hunting is tough. New Yorker Bill Vaznis, a well-known outdoor writer and accomplished whitetail bow-hunter, makes a habit of taking a nice whitetail buck from the deep woods near his upstate home each year by still hunting. "I try and find the deer when they're up feeding, but I've also found them in their beds," Vaznis says. Vaznis knows the country intimately, which means he knows where the deer are likely to be before he ever begins. That gives him an advantage. In unfamiliar country, scouting can give you the confidence you need to still hunt effectively. When there's fresh sign around, you'll expect, not hope, to see game.

Vaznis is a careful still hunter, taking only a step or two before carefully scanning ahead with both his naked eye and his binoculars. He's looking for a piece of a deer, not the whole animal. He also listens carefully for the sound of a deer walking. He makes sure the wind is either in his face or blowing crossways. When the wind is swirling badly, he doesn't still hunt, knowing the odds are stacked against him. He makes sure he's wearing silent clothing, favoring wool over synthetic fabrics. If there is crunchy snow on the ground, the wind's wrong, or the leaves are dry and crackly, he hunts from a stand. But when it's cool enough for the deer to be moving, the ground is quiet, and the wind is steady enough to keep game from smelling him, Vaznis prefers still hunting to stand hunting. "Taking a deer this way is the most satisfying type of hunting I do," he says. "But things have to be just right or you're wasting your time."

CALLING

You can call a variety of big-game animals into bow range, including deer, elk, bears, pronghorns, and wild hogs. Calling is an exciting form of hunting in that it can offer all the advantages of stand hunting—basically, you're taking a stand while trying to bring the animals to your location—while still being a very active game.

There are two basic ways to approach game calling, says David Hale, half of the legendary Knight & Hale game-calling team and a superb bowhunter. "You can call blind, meaning you haven't seen an animal nearby but hope one hears you and comes in," Hales says. "Or you can first locate an animal, get close to it, then try and call it in for the shot."

Hale has successfully used a variety of calls to lure in deer, including grunt calls, doe bleats, and fawn distress calls. "Of the three, the grunt call is the best all-around call," he says. "Bucks will respond to it all season long, but it is especially effective during the rut. The doe bleat is the best early in the year and will draw in mostly does but also bucks that happen to be hanging around. Fawn distress calls, which are more squalls than quiet calls like grunts or bleats, simulate the sound of a fawn in trouble. Using them is a great way to bring in does, especially early in the year." Distress calls can also scare the dickens out of deer, so they should be used judiciously. Elk can be similarly called in, but instead of grunt and bleat calls hunters use bugles and cow calls.

Rattling can be an effective whitetail hunting tactic at times, especially during the rut.

Another method of calling that can work well on whitetail and blacktail deer, and occasionally on elk and mule, is antler rattling. This involves banging a set of antlers together to simulate two bucks or bulls fighting over a doe or cow. To that end, antlers are best employed during the rut, particularly the pre-rut period, before the actual mating begins in earnest.

"While I have rattled in my share of bucks, I have also seen negative reactions when rattling," Hale concludes. "But the grunt call is something else. I've never seen a deer noticeably spook from my grunting, and I've had several bucks not pay any attention to it, too, and just continue to walk on past. But I have had so many bucks change course and come into range in response to my grunt calls that I never head into the deer woods without one anymore."

MAKING THE SHOT

After all that time, practice, and effort, it's come together. A nice buck has just come into view. For some reason, your knees are knocking together, your palms are sweaty, and your body is shivering, even though it's 70 degrees out. How can that be?

The excitement, the anticipation of making the shot when bowhunting is an adrenaline rush that's hard to describe to those who have not experienced it. If it didn't happen, there would be little thrill to hunting at all. After 30 years and countless opportunities, I still get "the shakes." That's good. It means the inner fire still burns brightly. But it can also be bad. Learning to control your overactive adrenal glands is a big part of making the shot on game.

CONFIDENCE

You can't make the shot under pressure without confidence in both your equipment and your ability to use it. That's why you were so careful when you chose your bow, arrows, and accessories, took the time to meticulously tune your setup, then spent so much time practicing during the off-season, both on the target range and during the realistic field-shooting situations that simulate actual bowhunting.

It's important to note that accurate shooting is just one facet of a successful bow hunt. You have to be able to get close enough to your quarry, precisely estimate the distance to the target, and control the shakes (more commonly known as "buck fever") as well as shoot an accurate arrow to be able to place your tag on a deer.

There are no shortcuts. In bowhunting, there is no substitute for experience in all aspects of the game. In the beginning, you're going to make mistakes that cost you game. That's okay. Don't be afraid of those mistakes. Instead, use them as learning opportunities. You'll move at the wrong time, and a deer will nail you. You'll misjudge the range, and shoot over the buck's back. You'll forget about wind direction, and the deer will smell you and bound off. A million and one things can go wrong at any given moment when you're trying to make the shot on game. The more days you spend in the woods, the more times you're close to game, the more your confidence level will grow—to the point that when the deer you want finally shows itself, you're going to drill it.

MAXIMUM EFFECTIVE SHOOTING RANGE

Deciding when to turn an arrow loose is the most important decision a bowhunter can make. The whole philosophy behind ethical bowhunting is not just to shoot some arrows, but rather to take only high-percentage shots at calm animals that are both positioned properly and within your maximum effective shooting range.

Just as athletes competing in the same sport have different skill levels, each bowhunter has his or her own personal shooting ability. No one else shoots at game exactly the same way, or with the exact same degree of skills, as you do. No two bowhunters perceive, or even see, the target identically, even under the same conditions. It's an individual thing. One of the most important things in all of bowhunting is for each individual to recognize his own shooting abilities–and inabilities—and to stay within himself at all times.

Most game taken with bow and arrow is shot at 30 yards or less. After all, bowhunting is by its very nature a short-range, get-in-their-face game. But though they never talk about it in public, I know bowhunters who have taken game in the wide-open spaces of the West at 60 yards or more, their arrows slicing through the center of the animal's chest as neat as you please. These bowhunters are afraid to tell anyone how far their shots were, hoping to avoid others' accusing them of being poor sportsmen. In reality, these individuals have earned the right to take longer shots through constant practice; careful tuning of, and uncompromising confidence in, their bow-and-arrow setup; a familiarity

The best shot placement practice of all is to shoot at life-sized 3-D animal targets set at unknown distances. Practicing the type of shots you'll most likely face in the field, such as shooting from a tree stand if you hunt from one, will prepare you for success when you get that once-in-a-lifetime opportunity.

with the terrain they hunt; and an intimate knowledge of the habits of the animals they pursue. In fact, they have more right to take a 50-yard shot at game than many less-skilled bowhunters have in shooting half that distance.

You can determine your maximum effective shooting range (MESR) on the target range. Use either the kill zone on a life-sized 3-D target or an eight-inch paper plate—which is about the size of the average deer's heart/lung area—as your target. Shoot your broadheads from farther and farther back until you quit placing all your arrows inside the bull's eye. When you begin missing, you're past your MESR.

Remember that this is your MESR under ideal conditions, which are rarely replicated in the field. Each shot presents a unique set of problems that must be overcome, distance being only one of them. Rain, fog, steep uphill or downhill angle, thick brush, and other factors all must be taken into account when deciding whether or not to shoot.

On several of my bow hunts, poor light was the determining factor in my not taking the shot. On another occasion—a bedded mule deer buck on a grassy slope—the 30 yards my angle finder told me was the exact distance between us was in no way the reason I didn't shoot. A strong, gusting crosswind of perhaps 30 mph made it hard to steady my bow and would have pushed my arrow to the side a distance which I was unsure. To try to minimize the wind's effect, I tried to sneak closer. Impatience made me hurry, and at 20 yards I rolled a softball-sized rock right into the buck's back. Had I been pitching horseshoes I would have been a winner. Instead I had an excellent view of that 26-incher's backside as he bounded off into the timber.

Another often-overlooked factor in deciding whether or not to take the shot is the attitude of the animal. Is it calm or tense? Alert animals can literally "jump the string," a term used to describe the lightning-quick reflexes of deer and other animals that allow them to literally jump out of the way of your arrow before it arrives. It may be hard to believe that a whitetail can move fast enough to cause a complete miss at 20 yards, but high-speed photography has shown this to regularly be the case.

For that reason, you want to shoot only at calm animals. And that's another factor in the distance equation. For years I believed that getting the animal in close enough to literally reach out and touch it was the way to go. Then I learned about what I call a big-game animal's internal radar. It seems that whenever they get closer to me than 15 yards, they just sense something's up. Their acute senses can hear the slightest sound, their eyes will pick up the smallest movement, and they'll tense up, ready to jump at the slightest commotion. That's why I try to take the first good shot I can get between 20 and 30 yards. I don't want the animal any closer than that.

SHOT PLACEMENT

With a rifle or slug gun, it usually doesn't matter what angle the deer is standing at when it's time to shoot. The power of the projectile enables it to smash through bone and lots of heavy muscle into the vitals, and its shocking power can knock the animal literally off its feet. An arrow doesn't have that bone-smashing penetrating ability or shocking power, instead relying on massive hemorrhage or the collapse of the heart or lungs to dispatch the animal. Thus, there are two—and only two—acceptable shot angles: broadside or slightly quartering away.

These two angles offer the only trouble-free access to the deer's vital heart/lung region. Sending a razor-sharp broadhead through both lungs of even the biggest, toughest animal will drop it so quickly, it will amaze you. For example, I once shot a 700-pound Alaskan grizzly bear—one tough cookie—through both lungs at 35 yards. The bear spun around, bit at the entrance hole made by the razor-sharp blades of my broadhead, and sprinted off, falling graveyard dead in less than 30 seconds. However, animals hit in the wrong place with an arrow can run seemingly forever, making recovery difficult if not impossible.

Aiming for the lungs is the right shot in almost every instance. They present the animal's largest vital target and are bordered on three sides by other vitals—the spine above, liver behind, and heart below—giving you a little leeway. Where to aim? On broadside shots, as your vertical reference aim for the distinct vertical "crease" in the hair just below the animal's front leg; for your horizontal reference, aim about halfway up the chest cavity. When the animal is quartering slightly away from you, for your horizontal mark again aim halfway up the chest, but for the vertical mark aim for the opposite front leg. Don't take a shot if the animal is strongly quartering away, though, as your arrow could glance off a rib bone and deflect back away from the lungs and liver and into the paunch.

The best shots are at animals standing completely still. However, animals walking slowly offer good shots, too. You have to time the shot so that the front leg is moving forward and out of the way of your arrow when it arrives at the chest. Never shoot at running game, or animals directly facing at you, or facing directly away from you. The odds are too long that something will go wrong.

AFTER THE SHOT

Though you know you've made a perfect shot, the hunt is anything but over at the time of release. Until you've recovered the animal and put your tag on him you cannot consider it a successful ending. Despite a perfect hit, the animal will probably race off before falling. In the thick country where most game is arrowed, this means you are going to have to track him.

Though the adrenaline is rolling through your veins like the proverbial railroad train, there's much to do after the shot. Most important is to watch the animal for as long as possible, both to see its posture and where it goes. Visually mark a landmark at the spot near which it disappears. This will be helpful when taking up the trail.

It is also important to stay as quiet as possible. One of the advantages a bow has over a firearm is its silence, which generally does not spook an animal the way the loud report of a firearm will. Don't add to the animal's excitement by making unnecessary noise. Being quiet also helps you follow the animal with your ears. Unless the wind is blowing hard or there's a noisy stream nearby, I've heard the animal go down many times before ever leaving my stand.

Get control of yourself. Look at your watch and note the time. Mine has a built-in stop watch, which I click on immediately after the shot. This helps me know exactly how long it's been since the hit while I'm waiting to take up the trail. Use your compass to take a reading on the animal's direction of travel from your stand to the last place you saw it. This reference can be a big help, especially when you are hunting from an elevated tree stand, because the lay of the land always looks different from ground level.

Though I've been bowhunting a long time, I'm still amazed at how many times a well-hit animal leaves little in the way of a blood trail. Some blood trails are so easy to follow that a blind man could recover the animal. Other times the trail is so faint, Dick Tracy would have trouble putting it all together.

Some hits are teasers. Many non-lethal hits, such as a hit in the thick muscles of the leg, can result in a lot of blood for the first 25 to 75 yards, and then the trail disappears like a wisp of smoke on a strong breeze. It may then turn into the occasional drop of blood here and there, leading you on a fruitless tracking job that will last as long as you want to keep it up. Blood volume, while always encouraging, is not a definitive indicator that your hit was a lethal one.

For many years, the rule of thumb following a bow shot has been wait for at least 30 minutes before taking up the track. Generally speaking that's a good rule to follow. Even though the shot looked perfect to you, the animal may have jumped the string without your knowing it, causing the arrow to arrive slightly off-target.

Game that has been hit poorly will generally do one of two things. Those hit in the paunch area will run off, then move at a slow walk for 100 to 300 yards before lying down. Unless forced from its bed, an animal will usually remain in place until it dies. This means waiting at least overnight on an evening shot and until late afternoon or the next morning on a shot taken in early morning light.

Waiting long enough under these circumstances cannot be overemphasized. If you spook the animal and it runs another half-mile to a mile before bedding up again, your chances of recovering it drop dramatically. It will usually leave no blood to speak of, and following tracks is almost always impossible. Of course, all this assumes that weather conditions permit waiting. When it rains, you have to take up the track before Mother Nature washes away all the evidence.

On most game, your arrow will have passed clean through the animal. The shaft will usually be lying very close to the spot of the shot. Find it, and carefully examine it for blood, hair, and other signs that will tell you where the animal has been hit.

The best-case scenario is to locate an arrow covered with bright red, bubbly blood. This means a lung hit. Very dark red blood can mean a liver or kidney hit, but may also mean a leg hit. When this occurs, wait several hours before following. Greenish residue means a paunch hit. Wait as long as conditions allow when this occurs, but generally at least 12 hours. There will also be times when you can't find the arrow. This does not mean the hit was bad, only that you can't find the shaft. Forget about it, and search for blood sign.

Follow the trail alert and ready for anything. Move as quietly as you can. I always follow a blood trail as if I were still-hunting the spookiest deer. Try not to spook other animals that may give away your presence to game that is not yet dead. Avoid loud talking, banging equipment, or other unnecessary, boisterous noises.

As you follow the trail, mark it with the fluorescent flagging you should always carry in your hunting pack for just such an occasion. Toilet tissue will also work. You don't have to mark every speck of blood, but mark the trail often enough so that you can see the last flagged spot. (Be sure to go back and remove all your flagging after you're done.)

Look for blood splotches on branches and brush as well as on the ground. Also, watch for tracks, overturned leaves, and other signs of an animal passing through the area. I carry a small quarter-inch steel tape in my pack to measure the animal's track, in case I lose the blood trail and have to continue the job by following tracks alone. This helps me identify the target animal if its tracks get mixed up with those of other deer.

Success at the end of a blood trail is the sweetest feeling in the world. I only had to track this big Kansas whitetail for 75 yards.

The best trail often ends surprisingly, like a small creek vanishing into the desert floor. When that happens, mark the spot and make a tight circle of 10 to 20 yards as you try and pick it up again. If you find nothing, widen the circle. Use your head. Study the lay of the land, and try to guess where the animal has gone. There are no hard and fast rules when tracking game, but mortally hit animals will rarely go uphill; they will go sidehill and climb slight inclines, and almost always head for the thick stuff.

Get down on your hands and knees and look for the tiniest speck of blood on the bottom of a leaf that has been overturned by the animal's hoof. More than once I've picked up the track after losing a good blood trail that petered out by finding a single speck of blood many yards from the last good blood sign. When the blood trail begins to thin, it's time to use other tracking skills, such as following tracks themselves, in combination with intermittent blood specks. Take care not to obliterate blood sign by walking over it.

If the blood trail ends and you can't find any more signs, start searching for the animal itself. Now's the time to get others to help if they're available. If not, use your compass and map out a grid that you'll walk thoroughly. Leave no stone, log, gully, or brush pile unturned as you double- and triple-check all the possibilities, Don't give up until you've either found the animal or are 1,000 percent sure it's nowhere to be found.

GLOSSARY OF BOWHUNTING TERMS

Adjustable limbs. Bow limbs that provide the capability of draw weight and/or tiller adjustment.

Adjustment range. (a) In draw weight, the minimum to the maximum bow weight, expressed in pounds, over which the manufacturer recommends the bow be used. (b) In draw length, the longest to the shortest draw length capabilities for which the bow was designed.

AMO. Archery Manufacturers and Merchants Organization, the key trade group made up of manufacturers and marketers of archery and bowhunting equipment of all sizes.

AMO draw length. True draw length + 1¾ inches.

Anchor point. To draw the bowstring to the same location in relation to a consistent reference point at full draw.

Armguard. A piece of stiff material used to protect the bow arm from the slap of the bowstring upon release. Usually placed on the inside of the forearm.

Arrow. Projectile shot from a hand-held or crossbow, having a point on the forward end and fletching on the rear end.

Arrow length. The length of the shaft as measured from the bottom of the nock notch to the end of the shaft, not including the arrow point.

Arrow nock. A notch or groove in the end of the arrow shaft for receiving the bowstring. Modern nocks are made from plastic and are generally replaceable and adjustable.

Arrow rest. The means used to support the arrow while it is attached to the bowstring. Modern arrow rests are adjustable horizontally, vertically, and fore or aft for precise adjustment.

Arrow shelf. The horizontal offset in the bow handle immediately above the grip, usually formed by a sight window recess. Can be used as an arrow rest on convention recurve and long bows.

Arrow weight. The total weight of an arrow in grains, including fletching, nock, inserts and/or overserts, and arrow point (7,000 grains/pound).

Arrowhead. The tip of an arrow, designed to give the arrow proper balance and protect the front end of the shaft or to aid in penetration.

Axle. The shaft upon which a compound bow's wheels/cams pivot.

Axle-to-axle length. The distance measured from center to center of the two most distant axles on a compound bow in the undrawn state.

Bare bow (or barebow). The style of bow shooting that does not allow the use of sights or other aiming aids.

Bare shaft testing. The use of unfletched arrows at close range to aid in bow tuning.

Bast. The twisted and coiled straw back of a target matt to which the target face is attached.

Blade clearance. Design or condition of a bow handle permitting a broadhead blade to clear the handle without contact.

Blunt. An arrow tip that is not pointed, often used to hunt small game or in "stump-shooting" practice.

Bow arm. The arm that holds the bow while shooting.

Bow press. A device used to hold a bow in a bent position, with the pressure off the bowstring. Used for repair work, for safely working on the bow while adding accessories, and so on.

Bow sight. An aiming device that can be attached to the bow handle (riser) above the arrow rest to give one or more points of reference.

Bow square. A device, usually T-shaped, used to measure bowstring brace height and proper nocking height or location.

Bowstring. Usually multiple strands of a suitable material used to connect the bow limbs, and to launch the arrow.

Bow weight. Actual physical weight of the bow itself with no accessories mounted or attached. Also known as mass weight.

Bowyer. A bow maker.

Brace height. Dimension from the grip pivot point to the inside edge of the bowstring measured at 90 degrees with the bow in the undrawn condition.

Broadhead. Arrow tip with blades having cutting edges suitable for hunting.

Compound bow. A bow that uses a system of cams or levers, pulleys, and cables to control the force that an archer must apply as the bowstring is drawn. Peak weight usually occurs during the first half of the draw cycle, with a reduction in force at full draw.

Cable guard. A device used to hold cables aside to clear arrow fletching and prevent the cable from interfering with arrow flight during the shot sequence.

Cable slide. A device that attaches to the cable and prevents cable coating wear by isolating the cables from the cable guard.

Cam. General term for any eccentric wheel used on a compound bow that produces a draw force relationship that retains the peak weight for an extended period of the draw, thus increasing the amount of energy stored.

Center serving. The central section of the bowstring that has been wrapped with a protective material to prevent wear.

Center shot. (a) Left/right horizontal placement of the arrow rest in the sight window of the bow handle riser. (b) Can refer to the amount the sight window is offset in order to achieve ease of arrow shaft passage.

Cock feather. The odd-colored feather or vane on an arrow shaft, which is used to index the shaft when attached to the bowstring.

Creep. Letting the shaft move forward before release and after reaching full draw.

Crossbow. A bow assembly mounted on a stock and utilizing a trigger mechanism for holding the arrow at full draw and releasing it.

Cushion plunger. A spring-loaded device mounted through the bow handle riser against which the side of the arrow rests. Usually adjustable in both spring tension and degree of center shot, it is a popular arrow rest type for fingers shooters.

Deflex. A bow design in which the ends of the handle or the limbs at the fade-outs are angled toward the belly and toward the archer.

Deflex-reflex. A bow design in which the unbraced limbs angle toward the shooter, then reverse attitude, angling backward away from the shooter.

Delamination. The failure and separation of a glue joint or the plies in a laminated bow.

Draw. To pull the bowstring toward your anchor position.

Draw length. The distance at full draw from the nocking point to the low point of the grip is true draw length. The distance at full draw from the nocking point to a point 1¾ inches beyond the pivot point of the grip is AMO length.

Draw weight. The maximum level of force required to bring the bowstring to the full draw or cocked position.

Drawing arm. The arm that draws the bowstring.

Drop-away arrow rest. An arrow rest where the launcher arm literally "drops away" from the shaft when the string is released, which eliminates the problem of fletch clearance.

Dry fire. Shooting a bow or crossbow without an arrow or bolt. This is a dangerous practice, never recommended, that can result in bow failure and serious injury.

Eccentric. The mechanical leverage device, usually attached to each bow-limb tip of a compound bow, designed to control the way the limbs store energy and ultimately provide mechanical advantage in order to reduce the force required to hold the bow at full draw.

Fast Flite. Trade name of a high-strength synthetic material used for making bowstrings. Made from an extended-chain polyethylene material.

Ferrule. That part of a screw-in broadhead that holds the cutting blades.

Fiber-optic sight. Bow sight pins made of colored plastic that gather a high volume of available daylight, making the pin tip easier to see in low-light conditions than traditional metal sight pins.

Field point. Arrow point designed to help reduce glances or ricochets upon impact with the ground when field shooting. Also commonly refers to arrow points used in target shooting.

Finger release. When one's fingers, with or without a finger protection device such as a tab or glove, are placed directly on the bowstring for the purpose of drawing and releasing the arrow.

Fletch. A vane or feather used in multiples and attached to the rear of the arrow shaft to stabilize the shaft in flight.

Follow through. The consistency of the position of various body parts, such as the head, bow arm, and drawing hand after the release of the bowstring.

Force draw curve. The graph created by plotting draw force (vertical axis) against the draw length (horizontal axis) for a bow as it is drawn from brace height through full draw.

FPS. Feet per second, which is how arrow speed is usually measured.

Fulcrum point. The point of the bow limb beyond which it is free to flex, located at the pivot point of an adjustable limb butt.

Full draw. The condition of the bow when the bowstring has been drawn and the draw hand is at the anchor point, or the position of a bow when drawn to its prescribed maximum draw length.

Handle. The section of a bow between the limbs.

Handle length. On a compound bow, the distance between the upper-limb fulcrum pivot point and lower-limb fulcrum pivot point.

Helical fletching. Fletching applied in a helical pattern, with vanes or feathers forming a helix around the shaft. Broadhead-tipped shafts generally fly best with helical fletching.

Hen feathers. On a three-fletched shaft, the two feathers opposed to the different-colored cock feather.

Instinctive shooting. A method of shooting in which no formal aiming method is used and the archer simply looks at the target and shoots "instinctively."

Kisser button. A marker permanently attached to the bowstring so that it touches the archer's lips at full draw. Used to help consistently anchor the bow.

Let-off. Difference between the peak draw weight and the actual holding weight divided by the peak weight, expressed as a percentage.

Limb. The major flexing portion of the bow attached above and below the center handle section. The limbs are flexed as the bowstring is drawn and are the means of storing the energy needed to propel the arrow.

Limb bolt. Bolt that attaches a limb to the handle and is often used to adjust both bow draw weight and limb tiller.

Limb butt. That portion of the limb that attaches to the bow handle.

Limb length. Determined in two ways: (a) the overall length of the limb along the limb surface, or (b) the length from the fulcrum point to the centerline of the axle.

Longbow. Straight one-piece or takedown bow.

Nock locator. An attachment to the center serving of the bowstring used to consistently position the end of the arrow. Also called a "nock set."

Nock throat. The notched part of an arrow nock that holds the shaft on the bowstring.

Nock height. The vertical distance measured on the bowstring from a line perpendicular to the string from the arrow rest level to the bottom of the nock.

Nocking point. The location at which the arrow is placed on the bowstring.

Outsert. An external adapter used to permit attachment of point or nock to an arrow shaft. Usually used with small-diameter carbon shafts.

Overbowed. Term used to describe an archer with a bow too great in draw weight to allow him to shoot properly.

Paper tuning. The use of paper, usually newspaper or butcher paper, mounted on a rectangular frame, for the purpose of recording the position of the point and nock ends of the arrow shaft as it passes through the plane of the paper.

Peak weight. (a) The maximum draw weight during the draw cycle, or (b) the maximum draw weight recommended by the manufacturer.

Peep sight. Any see-through aperture used for the purpose of aligning the bowstring with the front sight while at full draw, thus providing a three-dimensional sighting system. Also called a peep or string peep. Peeps are usually inserted between the strands of the bowstring above the nock point and held in place with waxed string.

Plunger hole. The threaded hole in the bow handle for mounting an adjustable arrow rest or cushion plunger.

Powder test. The use of a white spray or talc powder on the fletched end of the shaft or the arrow rest area of the bow handle to determine if there is contact between the fletching and arrow rest upon launch of the arrow.

Quiver. A device for holding a quantity of arrows. Can be attached to the bow or be of a design that is worn by the archer, usually on the back or the hip.

Recurve limb. A limb design in which the unbraced limb tips bend toward the back of the bow.

Reflex. A bow design in which the ends of the handle or the limbs at the fade-outs angle toward the back of the bow.

Relaxed weight. The holding weight of a compound bow in the fully drawn position.

Release. To shoot an arrow.

Release aid. A hand-held mechanical device that is temporarily attached to the bowstring and used to draw and release the string.

Riser. See "Handle."

Scope. An optical setting device, usually magnifying, used on a bow. Scopes are usually on target bows and are often illegal for bowhunting.

Serving. The act or result of wrapping a bowstring with an appropriate material to prevent wear. Commonly done at the center section and/or loop ends of the string.

Shaft. The body or main section of the arrow, extending between the nock and the point.

Shaft size. A designation given to a specific arrow size to allow ease of selection and matching to a particular bow weight and draw length.

Shoot-around rest. An arrow rest that requires that the shaft spine be such that the bottommost fletch of the arrow will pass to the outside of the support arm of the rest as it leaves the bow.

Shoot-through rest. An arrow rest in which the fletching clears any support for the arrow with minimum regard for the arrow spine.

Sight bar. A pin-like reference point, usually attached to a mounting and used to aim the arrow.

Sight window. Area of the handle offset from the limb centerline for the purpose of arrow passage, viewing the sighting apparatus, and obtaining a clear view of the target.

Sling. A device that allows the archer to shoot the bow with a relaxed bow hand grip. The sling prevents the bow from dropping from the bow hand immediately after release.

Spine. (a) The amount of bend (deflection) in an arrow shaft that is caused by a specific weight being placed at the center of the shaft while the shaft is supported at a designated span. (b) The recovery characteristics of an arrow that permit it to bend and recover to its original shape in flight.

Stabilizer. Any device added to the bow for the specific purpose of reducing handle torque and/or maintaining bow handle position during the shot. Stabilizers add inertia to the system, thereby increasing stability.

Stops. That portion of the draw cycle beyond the valley center or beyond the lowest holding weight, where attempting to draw the bow further results in an extremely rapid gain in draw weight. Also referred to as the "wall."

Stored energy. The amount of energy required to bring the bow limbs to full draw.

Straight limbs. Limbs that are not curved.

String hand. The hand that holds the bowstring or release aid during the draw.

String grooves. The two ends of the bow where the bowstring is fitted.

String loop. A small piece of small-diameter cord tied above and below the nocking point and to which a release aid is attached. The string loop replaces the nock set, reducing wear on the bowstring and helping make the release quieter. Also called a release rope.

String wax. A protective coating, usually beeswax, periodically rubbed onto the bow string to both condition and protect the string itself.

Swaging. The tapered shaping of the ends of an aluminum arrow shaft that will directly accept an arrow point or arrow nock, which are glued on.

Takedown bow. Any bow that is designed to come apart in the handle area, usually into two or three parts.

Tiller. Term used to describe the amount that the top handle/limb junction-to-string dimension is different from the bottom handle/limb junction-to-string dimension.

Tune. To adjust (with the proper arrow being used) the arrow rest, pressure point, string height, draw height, and nocking height to achieve optimum bow flight.

Underbowed. Term used to describe an archer with a bow with too little draw weight for the purpose intended.

Valley. The zone of lowest holding weight when a compound bow is drawn to the recommended draw position.

Vane. Synthetic fletching that replaces feathers on most modern arrows.

Wall. The region where rapid weight increase on the bowstring is reached when drawing a compound beyond the valley. Also referred to as the stops.

Weight adjustment. The ability to adjust the draw weight on a compound bow.

Whisker biscuit. An arrow rest with stiff synthetic fibers set in a full circle with a hole in the center just large enough for the arrow shaft to fit in. The fibers hold the arrow securely in place until the shot, when the arrow and its fletching simply shoot right through the fibers with no real loss in accuracy.

Windage. The left-right adjustment of the bow sight to the sight pin on a bow sight.

INDEX

Italicized page references indicate illustrations.

pendulum sights, 32–33
pin guards, 33–34
Pint, Norman, 18
Pope & Young Club, 4
portable tree stands, 91
practicing, 76–79, 84–85, *107*
prong-type arrow rests, 19, 24
pro shops, archery, viii–ix, 14
PSE-CF-TM Hunter (arrow rest), 20
PSE Hunter Supreme (arrow
    rest), 20

quartering away (shot angle),
    109, 110
quivers, *62,* 62–63

radios, compact, 94
range finders, 63–65, *64*
rattling, *103,* 104
recovery, animal, 110–14
recurve bows (traditional bows),
    2–3, 18
regulations, hunting, 31, 53–54
relaxation and shooting, 76
release aids
  finger tabs, 57–58
  mechanical, 58–61, *59*
  user statistics, 21
release shooting, 83
replaceable-blade broadheads,
    50–51, 52
ropes, pull, 93
rutting, 99

safety gear, 93
A Sand Country Almanac
    (Leopold), 87
saws, compact, 93
scents, masking, 96
senses, animal, 88, 96
shakes (buck fever), 24, 106
shears, pruning, 93
shooting
  bad habit development, 76, 77

confidence and, 105–6
maximum effective shooting
    range, 106–9
practice, 76–79, 84–85
relaxation and, 76
shot placement, *107,* 109–10
steps for, 79–84
shoot-through arrow rests, 20, 22
shot distances, 107, 109
shot placement, 109–10, 112
sight pins, 30–31, 81–82
sights
  crosshair, 31
  fixed-pin, 29–31, *30*
  movable-pin, 31–32
  peep (kisser buttons), 28, 28–29, 81
  pendulum, 32–33
slings, tree, 92
smell, sense of, 88, 96
Spectra, 11
spine, 38
spin tests, 73
split-limb bows, 9–10
spot and stalk hunting, 100–101
springy arrow rests, 19
stabilizers, 12–13, *14*
stadia wire guards, 33–34
stalking, 100–101
stance, 79–80, 80–81
stand hunting, 97–100
still hunting, 101–2
stretch, 10
strings, 10–12, 61, 83
stump shooting, 84
Styrofoam targets, 65–66
swaging, 39

tags, hunting, 94
talc-filled puff bottles, 94, *97*
targets, 65–66, 82, 85, *107,* 108
thermals, 101
three-dimensional targets, 66, 85
tillers, 69
timing shots, 11